TD
169
523
1995

California Maritime Academy Library (CSU)

D0871830

## DATE DUE

| | |
|---|---|
| | |
| | |
| | |
| | |
| | |
| | |
| | |
| | |
| | |
| | |
| | |
| | |
| | |
| | |
| | |
| | |
| | |
| GAYLORD | PRINTED IN U.S.A. |

WITHDRAWN

# Eco-Justice: Linking Human Rights and the Environment

WITHDRAWN

AARON SACHS

LIBRARY
CALIFORNIA MARITIME ACADEMY
P. O. BOX 1392
VALLEJO, CA 94590

Jane A. Peterson, *Editor*

WORLDWATCH PAPER 127
December 1995

**THE WORLDWATCH INSTITUTE** is an independent, nonprofit environmental research organization in Washington, D.C. Its mission is to foster a sustainable society in which human needs are met in ways that do not threaten the health of the natural environment or future generations. To this end, the Institute conducts interdisciplinary research on emerging global issues, the results of which are published and disseminated to decision makers and the media.

**FINANCIAL SUPPORT** is provided by the Nathan Cummings Foundation, the Energy Foundation, the Geraldine R. Dodge Foundation, the George Gund Foundation, W. Alton Jones Foundation, John D. and Catherine T. MacArthur Foundation, Andrew W. Mellon Foundation, Edward John Noble Foundation, Pew Charitable Trust, Lynn R. and Karl E. Prickett Fund, Rockefeller Brothers Fund, Surdna Foundation, Turner Foundation, U.N. Population Fund, Wallace Genetic Foundation, and Frank Weeden Foundation.

**PUBLICATIONS** of the Institute include the annual *State of the World*, which is now published in 27 languages; *Vital Signs*, an annual compendium of global trends that are shaping our future; the *Environmental Alert* book series; *World Watch* magazine; and the Worldwatch Papers. For more information on Worldwatch publications, write: Worldwatch Institute, 1776 Massachusetts Ave., NW, Washington, DC 20036; or fax 202-296-7365; or see back pages.

**THE WORLDWATCH PAPERS** provide in-depth, quantitative and qualitative analysis of the major issues affecting prospects for a sustainable society. The Papers are written by members of the Worldwatch Institute research staff and reviewed by experts in the field. Published in five languages, they have been used as concise and authoritative references by governments, nongovernmental organizations, and educational institutions worldwide. For a partial list of available Papers, see back pages.

**DATA** from all graphs and tables contained in this Paper are available on 3 1/2" Macintosh or IBM-compatible computer disks. The disks also include data from the *State of the World* series, *Vital Signs*, *Environmental Alert* book series, Worldwatch Papers, and *World Watch* magazine. Each yearly subscription includes a mid-year update, and *Vital Signs* and *State of the World* as they are published. The disk is formatted for Lotus 1-2-3, and can be used with Quattro Pro, Excel, SuperCalc, and many other spreadsheets. To order, see back pages.

© Worldwatch Institute, 1995
Library of Congress Catalog Number 95-061583
ISBN 1-878071-29-7

Printed on 100-percent non-chlorine bleached, partially recycled paper

# Table of Contents

Sections of this paper may be reproduced in magazines and newspapers
with written permission from the Worldwatch Institute. For information,
call the Director of Communication at (202)452-1999 or Fax: (202)296-7365.

The views expressed are those of the author and do not necessarily repre-
sent those of the Worldwatch Institute, its directors, officers, or staff, or of
its funding organizations.

**ACKNOWLEDGMENTS:** The entire Worldwatch Institute staff contributed to this project. My colleagues' skills improved this paper considerably, and their willingness to play softball once a week from May to September helped keep me (relatively) sane. I would especially like to thank Lori Baldwin and Laura Malinowski of our Library Staff for providing a steady flow of books and articles; Denise Byers Thomma and Jim Perry of our Communication Department for coordinating production and outreach; and Jennifer Seher for handling layout and making our transition to desktop publishing a smooth one. Payal Sampat and Suzanne Hollander contributed useful research summaries and insightful data analysis for the section on international environmental injustices. Every member of the Institute's Research Staff read some earlier version of this paper and offered helpful suggestions, as did outside reviewers Patricia Armstrong, Barbara Johnston, Michael Kane, Bill Loker, Lou Masur, Stephen Mills, Patti Petesch, Neil Popovic, and Jacob Scherr—and I am extremely grateful to all of them. I would also like to thank Hilary French, Christopher Flavin, and Ed Ayres for providing valuable project oversight. Finally, I want to dedicate this paper to the memory of Ken Saro-Wiwa, the playwright, Nobel Peace Prize nominee, and environmental justice activist who was executed by the Nigerian government on November 10, 1995, just as this paper was going to press.

**AARON SACHS**, Research Associate at the Worldwatch Institute, studies issues in international development, human rights, and the social and environmental impacts of technology. He has written articles on topics ranging from men's roles in family planning to the role of the environment in the Middle East peace talks. Sachs is co-author of Worldwatch Paper 121, *The Next Efficiency Revolution: Creating a Sustainable Materials Economy*, and co-author of two of the Institute's *State of the World* reports, among other publications. He is a graduate of Harvard University, where he studied history, literature, and the environment.

# Introduction: Human Rights and the Environment

"We demand a development policy for the Amazon that addresses the interests of rubber tappers and respects our rights. We do not accept an Amazonian development policy that favors large entrepreneurs who exploit and massacre workers and destroy nature."

> — *Platform of the National Rubber Tappers' Council,*
> *at the first Amazonian Rubber Tappers' Meeting,*
> *Brasilia, October 1985*[1]

Until just a few years before his murder in 1988, Chico Mendes, the Brazilian known internationally for the battle he waged against Amazonian deforestation, considered himself solely a social justice activist. His principal aim was to protect his fellow rubber tappers' right to earn a livelihood from the forest. Once he encountered the environmental movement, however, in 1985, Mendes realized that the international struggle to save the rain forest and his local struggle to empower its inhabitants amounted to nearly the same thing. That realization lies at the heart of his legacy: he showed that human rights and environmental issues are inextricably bound together. And the Chico Mendes Extractive Reserve, a tract of close to one million hectares of protected rain forest, stands as a testament to what can be accomplished when human rights activists and environmentalists acknowledge their commonality and join forces.[2]

Mendes's assassination—masterminded by a land-hungry cattle rancher—was most fundamentally a criminal act and a personal tragedy. But it also pointed to a much larger pattern of human rights abuse. An Amnesty International report revealed that there were more than a thousand land-related murders in rural Brazil in the 1980s, and fewer than ten convictions. Law enforcement officials made virtually no effort to protect civil liberties—such as the right to speak out and organize protests—because they shared the rancher's opinion that anyone who objected to the cutting and burning of the rain forest represented merely an obstacle to progress. The legal injustices Amnesty uncovered, then, were meant to reinforce the even more far-reaching injustices of rural development, the human rights abuses perpetrated against the entire community of forest dwellers.[3]

In Mendes's home state of Acre, in 1970, three-quarters of the land was publicly owned, technically unclaimed and undeveloped. By 1980, almost all of it had been bought, and about half was concentrated in the hands of only ten people. By doling out massive financial incentives to ranchers and speculators interested in developing the Amazon, the Brazilian government forced the scattered inhabitants of the rain forest to pay the price of deforestation—ranging from air pollution to the spread of disease to flooding and soil erosion—while a few wealthy land barons reaped most of the rewards.[4]

Environmental degradation, even in areas that seem remote, usually carries a high human cost. And, as Mendes pointed out, that cost is often borne disproportionately by the people least able to cope with it—people already on the margins of society. Thanks to Mendes, Amnesty International activists in rural Brazil realized that they needed help from the environmental movement—because many of the human rights abuses they were documenting were being driven by the pressure to cut and burn the rain forest. And environmentalists working in the Amazon learned from Mendes that one of the best ways of preventing deforestation was to use the human rights approach—to reform the law enforcement system and empower people to mount protests to defend their health and livelihoods.[5]

The sorts of issues that link the human rights and environmental agendas—largely involving unfair distribution of the costs of ecological damage and inequitable access to ecological benefits—are often referred to as environmental injustices. Though difficult to quantify or even document in some cases, because they are often associated with illegal activities, environmental injustices arise at all levels of society, affecting individuals, communities, and entire countries. Attacks against grassroots environmentalists—ranging from the bombing of forest service offices in the western United States to the official execution of activists in Nigeria—do occasionally grab headlines. But much of the suffering such activists struggle to prevent still goes largely unnoticed.[6]

Each year, construction schemes involving roads and dams displace more than ten million people from their homes, and industrial countries export millions of tons of hazardous waste to their poorer neighbors. An ongoing dam project in India's Narmada Valley has resulted in the forced relocation of thousands of tribal people, and gold-mining operations have poisoned the drinking water in several of the black South African homelands. Countless other projects sponsored by governments or corporations still threaten other communities all around the world.[7]

In the case of the Brazilian Amazon, the government's decision to set aside a portion of the rain forest for the rubber tappers' use has helped protect the tappers' human rights and has also encouraged sustainable development practices. The intact forest ecosystem can support a sizable population of highly productive tappers, who are eager to monitor it and keep it intact so that they can go on earning a living by gathering nuts and extracting latex from rubber trees. But each instance of environmental human rights abuse will require a different solution. During various local campaigns, activists fighting for what they call environmental justice have attempted to define their goal by explaining that protection from pollution and access to natural resources should be equalized—rather than reserved for those who can afford to live in the safest suburban communities or to buy up large tracts of rain forest. Yet in practice "equality" is just as vague a term as justice. The key to work-ing toward environmental justice, then, may be ensuring that the people in power cannot monopolize the right to determine what it means.[8]

As human rights activists well know, the best way of holding those who wield power accountable is through the protection of the basic civil and political freedoms—free speech, a free press providing access to information, fair elections, and freedom to organize in groups. Indeed, the worst cases of localized damage to the environment often occur in countries under the control of authoritarian, rights-repressive regimes, because affected communities have no way of mounting protests. Environmental protection was so difficult in the former Soviet Union, for instance, because concerned citizens could not build coalitions, or expose the government's shortcomings in the media, or vote uncooper-ative politicians out of office. Although major environmen-tal policy reforms are essential in halting ecological damage, then, guaranteeing the implementation of such reforms will ultimately depend on the full protection of basic human rights—especially those of society's most vulnerable people.[9]

Fortunately, the environmental and human rights movements have substantial common ground on which to build further linkages. In particular, both have traditionally focused on expanding access to information and upholding the right of communities to participate in decisions likely to affect their well-being. The two movements together could well gain enough influence to weave this approach into standard development policies. If more projects emphasized the full, well-informed involvement of local peoples, gov-ernments could no longer treat them—or their environ-ments—as expendable. And if there were no expendable people or ecosystems, development would have to be sus-tainable. Environmental justice campaigns are not just try-ing to spread out the costs of environmental damage more equitably—they are trying to reduce the overall amount of environmental damage.[10]

# What Greenpeace and Amnesty International Are Learning from Each Other

"I know no safe depository of the ultimate powers of the society but the people themselves; and if we think them not enlightened enough to exercise their control with a wholesome discretion, the remedy is not to take it from them, but to inform their discretion."

— *Thomas Jefferson, letter to William Charles Jarvis, September 28, 1820*[11]

In recent years, environmentalists and human rights workers have joined forces in many local struggles over land and water rights, toxic dumping, and disruptive construction projects. But much of the potential of this budding coalition is still unrealized, because these local campaigns have not yet organized themselves into prominent national or international networks or umbrella groups—a growing necessity, especially because so many environmental justice issues are global in nature. Moreover, while many environmentalists have embraced environmental justice concerns, some of their potential allies in the human rights movement have hesitated to stray too far from their traditional focus—on cases involving prisoners of conscience, fair trial, torture, and the death penalty. The two sets of activists still have a lot to learn from each other. But the considerable overlap of their agendas, on such issues as environmental health hazards and threats to indigenous peoples' resource bases, should continue to bring the two movements together.[12]

In view of this overlap, it is not surprising that environmental and human rights workers have been collaborating for years at the grassroots level. As Ashish Kothari, Lecturer in Environmental Studies at the Indian Institute of Public Administration, has noted: "Most mass movements at the grassroots are not just human rights, nor just environmental, but inevitably both. They have to be, if they are conscious of the role of natural resources in their lives, and of the dominant forces exploiting those resources." A broad coalition of local activists in northern India, for instance,

has mounted one of the most effective environmental justice campaigns in the world. Since 1973, protests by the
famous tree-huggers of the Chipko movement have slowed
deforestation considerably. The government's auctioning of
forests to earn foreign exchange, the activists pointed out,
had come at the expense of local peoples, who suffered from
increased flooding, siltation of their irrigation systems, and
diminished fuelwood supplies.[13]

In the United States, the first activists to organize themselves under the environmental justice rubric actually came
out of the civil rights movement. Such groups as the United
Church of Christ's Commission for Racial Justice, Oakland's
Center for Third World Organizing, and even the U.S. government's General Accounting Office (GAO) generated studies in the mid-1980s documenting the link between high
concentrations of minorities and high concentrations of
pollution. The United Church of Christ's 1987 study, for
instance, researched all 415 of the hazardous waste facilities
then in existence in the United States and determined that
people of color were about twice as likely as white people to
live in the towns that hosted such facilities. By the 1990s,
grassroots activists fighting institutional racism had realized
how much they had in common with grassroots activists
fighting the use of toxic chemicals, and the two groups were
beginning to collaborate relatively frequently.[14]

At the international level, joint projects have proceeded
much more gradually. But the largest international environmental and human rights organizations of the North have
made at least a few attempts at collaboration, both with
each other and with smaller campaigns and organizations in
the South. The list of groups that have worked with rubber
tappers' and indigenous peoples' organizations in the
Brazilian Amazon, for instance, ranges from Amnesty
International to the World Wildlife Fund. The broader the
coalition, they all have begun to realize, the more its policy
agendas take on universal relevance, and the more political
power it attains. In April, 1992, the Yale Law School hosted
a conference on "Earth Rights and Responsibilities: Human

Rights and Environmental Protection." Later that year, Human Rights Watch and the Natural Resources Defense Council together released a report entitled *Defending the Earth: Abuses of Human Rights and the Environment*, which documented some of the most vicious attacks against environmental activists. Then, in October 1995, the Sierra Club and Amnesty International issued their first joint letter, which dealt with the link between human rights abuses and environmental degradation in Nigeria.[15]

Even these notable efforts to collaborate have been quite cautious, however. Decades of fostering very different approaches to advocacy have led to a certain amount of mutual distrust. Members of Amnesty International, for instance, famous for their letter-writing campaigns on behalf of individual prisoners of conscience, have tended to feel little sympathy for eco-philosophers trying to make a case for "the rights of nature." They have difficulty understanding why some ecologists might be willing to spend so much energy on efforts to prevent the possible future extinction of an obscure species of bird, for instance, supposedly for the eventual good of everyone—while human beings are being tortured right here in the present. Similarly, ecologists have tended to grow exasperated with the narrow human-rights focus on single cases of abuse, pointing out that far more people are threatened by such things as desertification and water pollution than by torture.[16]

**The study determined that people of color were twice as likely as white people to live near hazardous waste facilities.**

Some of the lingering hesitancy on the part of human rights activists to tackle environmental justice issues stems from a historical split within their own movement. Ever since the United Nations' General Assembly adopted the Universal Declaration of Human Rights, in 1948, human rights have been thought of as falling into two separate categories: individual civil liberties, ranging from free speech to freedom from torture; and the broader, more communal rights to such things as health, food, shelter, and work. Though the Universal Declaration itself is not a binding legal document, in later years both sets of rights did enter into force as binding international laws, in the Covenant on Civil and Political Rights and the broader Covenant on Economic, Social, and Cultural Rights. The mandates of many prominent human rights organizations focus them almost exclusively on civil and political rights—the so-called rights of the person—mainly because they are easier to define and enforce. Some leaders have argued for a broadening of their advocacy to include the active defense of economic, social, and cultural rights—the rights that tend to be at the core of environmental justice issues. But many others have insisted that taking on the second set of rights would in the end weaken the effectiveness of the movement as a whole.[17]

Working for the recognition of a new communal right to a "healthy and healthful environment" need not require the human rights movement to abandon its traditional approach, however. Indeed, environmentalists are increasingly recognizing that one of the best ways to guarantee the enjoyment of communal environmental rights is by upholding the basic civil and political rights of the individual. In the environmental justice context, then, the distinction between the relevant civil and political rights and the relevant economic, social, and cultural rights perhaps reveals more of a complementarity than a conflict. The first set of rights are largely procedural, and the second are substantive: people can use their individual rights (such as free speech) to protect their environment-related communal rights (the right to an ozone layer). Both the human rights movement and the environmental movement are inevitably fighting for both sets of rights.[18]

With regard to the environment, substantive, communal rights would uphold global interdependence and the protection of life: they would establish ecological standards, laying out the things all people as a society should be able to expect from the environment, such as clean air and water; and they would explain just what would constitute an environmental injustice. But it is the existing procedural rights that provide the most common ground for the two movements, at the individual, communal, and even national level, because all human rights activists already recognize them as their top priorities. And environmentalists are willing to grant these rights primacy as well, because they are the ones that allow people to work toward the *prevention* of environmental injustices.[19]

Still another group of human rights activists remain reluctant to work on environmental justice issues, however, because at times environmentalists really have neglected the human element of conservation. As Osmarino Amâncio Rodrigues, a friend of Chico Mendes, put it, "They didn't realize there were human beings in the forest." The campaign to preserve wilderness areas, in particular, which is the branch of environmentalism with the longest tradition, has occasionally strayed quite far from any social consciousness. Just as entrepreneurial farmers and ranchers have sometimes cleared land without regard to its inhabitants, some environmentalists have set aside large areas as inviolable wildlife preserves without making arrangements for the local people who had depended on that land for their livelihoods for generations. Several badly planned ecological preservation projects, in other words, have come at the expense of local inhabitants' basic human rights. And such mismanagement, in turn, often jeopardizes the integrity of the supposedly protected areas.[20]

**Several badly planned ecological preservation projects have come at the expense of local inhabitants' human rights.**

This pattern has been especially devastating in the developing world. In Kenya, for instance, the setting aside of wilderness preserves such as Amboseli National Park has forced the pastoralist Masai people to abandon some of their traditional homelands, which have since deteriorated quite rapidly despite their protected status. The Masai and their cattle had played an integral role in fending off scrub growth and sustaining the rich Serengeti grasslands. In many protected areas of India as well, local peoples have found themselves suddenly deprived of traditional lands and access to natural resources because of new conservation regulations, and they have responded, understandably, with increasing hostility. The creation of the Kutru Tiger and Buffalo Reserve in Madhya Pradesh, for instance, displaced 52 villages of Maria tribals, many of whom have since joined an insurgent movement that occasionally conducts poaching missions and harasses park guards.[21]

Because of such failures, and because so many developing-world preservation schemes originate with industrial-world environmental organizations, northern environmentalists have constantly had to fend off accusations that they care more about the South's trees and birds than about its people. "Just because these people say that they are helping the environment," insists one Tyua woman in western Zimbabwe, "does not mean that they should be able to violate our human rights." In addition, many preservationist recommendations coming from the North have been criticized as hypocritical because the industrial countries have already harvested many of their own natural resources and show no signs of being willing to reduce their consumption.[22]

Over the last five to ten years, however, as environmentalists learned to address the social and cultural context of their campaigns, they became better able to demonstrate the immediate human value of intact ecosystems. While large groups like Greenpeace and the Environmental Defense Fund lent their political clout to small, local human rights campaigns, Indians and rubber tappers emerged from the forest to attend international environmental conferences and give ecology a human face. The North's aloof tree-lovers became compassionate defenders of local peoples.[23]

The human rights approach is not a fool-proof environmental strategy, however. Sometimes an exclusively rights-based approach to protecting local peoples has in fact opened the door to increased environmental degradation, which in turn tends to erode the peoples' basic rights and well-being. Along the coasts of Ecuador's Galápagos Islands, for instance, empowered local fishers are currently overharvesting sea cucumbers at a rate likely to wipe out supplies within about four years. By embracing the international economy and selling their bounty to wealthy gourmets in China and Japan, the cucumber fishers, known as *pepineros*, are able to make up to 20 times the profit they could earn from any other locally available species.[24]

The original plan establishing the Galápagos National Park in 1974 pointedly protected indigenous peoples' right to continue their tradition of subsistence fishing. But Ecuadoran officials subsequently failed to distinguish between indigenous peoples and new residents of the islands. Many of the commercial *pepineros* moved to the Galápagos region just a few years ago, specifically to collect sea cucumbers. Moreover, Ecuador's government has made no attempt to implement any monitoring mechanisms by which it could ensure that the Galápagueños are keeping their fishing within subsistence levels. As the native Galápagueño ecologist Carlos A. Valle has noted, the *pepineros*, who have gone so far as to take hostages in their fight to keep the fishery open, seem to be intent on defending their "right to destroy their own future."[25]

Similarly, the Kayapó Indians of the Brazilian Amazon have recently begun to make illegal deals with loggers and miners, allowing for large-scale extraction of mahogany and gold on their lands. Less than a decade ago, after the Kayapó had staged several highly publicized protests to demand land rights, the Brazilian government granted them a 65,000-square-kilometer reserve from which timber and mining companies were barred by law, for the Indians' own protection. But since then several Kayapó chiefs have decided to cash in timbering and mining privileges for various luxury items, ranging from satellite dishes to cars and private jets. Most of the tribe members, meanwhile, live in poverty and lack basic health care, and the influence of outsiders has eroded many traditional livelihoods and cultural practices. Moreover, the newly introduced extractive industries constitute a public health threat: more than half of the inhabitants of the village of Gorotire, for instance, whose chiefs decided to allow gold mining on their land, have unsafe levels of mercury in their blood, thanks to the miners' ore-processing techniques.[26]

Both the region's ecological integrity and the Kayapó's cultural integrity, then, are collapsing under the pressures of the international economy and its demand for gold jewelry and tropical hardwoods. Of course, the Kayapó have a right to control their own destiny; but they also have a responsibility to abide by the law and honor their commitment to sustainable land use. And the Brazilian government likewise has a responsibility to enforce its laws.

Environmentalists will never meet their goals without respecting the rights of local peoples. At the same time, however, they and human rights activists alike need to realize that their efforts cannot cease once rights have been established. As Thomas Jefferson asserted, if people are not exercising their power in a socially responsible manner, then it is the duty of society to suggest alternative approaches. One of the most important functions of environmental justice campaigns is to enable the communities they defend to develop in an environmentally sustainable way.

The demands of conservation may seem to conflict with the rights of the *pepineros* and the Kayapó; yet conservationists could make a strong case that better environmental regulation and monitoring would in the long run strengthen the rights of both communities. Indeed, if the *pepinero* community were comprised of more indigenous peoples, who naturally have a deeper investment in the local ecosystem than outsiders do, the fishers might actually desire limits on sea cucumber harvests as long-term protection for their natural resource base. And if the Kayapó had not already been experiencing the intrusions of government-sponsored development for several years, they too might have chosen not to cash in so many of their natural resources. In general, when human rights and ecology are given equal weight and local people not only participate in the development decisions that are going to affect them but also have a strong ecological knowledge base, communities end up acting as stewards of the local environment. They are then in a position to flourish socially and culturally as well as economically.[27]

**Environmentalists will never meet their goals without respecting the rights of local peoples.**

Again, the case of the Amazonian rubber tappers, who have successfully defended their land from most fires and chain saw crews, provides a good illustration of just how much environmentalists and human rights activists can accomplish by working together. It was a core group of ecologists, anthropologists, human rights workers, and labor leaders, collaborating both in small Amazonian communities and in Washington, D.C., that came up with the solution of extractive reserves—a system that makes the mutual interdependence of the people and the land into a positive binding force. This alliance did not prevent the murder of Chico Mendes or halt the destruction of the rainforest. But as a result of its efforts the rubber tappers and Indians of Acre now have more protection than ever before, and the pace of local deforestation has slowed considerably since the mid-1980s.[28]

On extractive reserves throughout the region, tappers and other local peoples harvest and market between ten and fifteen different products, ranging from rubber and nuts and oils to crops such as cocoa, coffee, and pepper, which grow well in the shade of the forest canopy. In Xapuri, Chico Mendes's home town, the local tappers' cooperative, with the help of a U.S. non-profit firm called Cultural Survival

Enterprises, developed links with one of the world's most powerful ice cream companies, Ben and Jerry's Homemade. For a few years the co-op's workers received a small percentage of the profit whenever northern consumers put a spoonful of Rainforest Crunch ice cream to their lips. Thanks to those profits, the tappers now have their own nut-processing plant, which as of the early 1990s was Xapuri's biggest employer.[29]

To be sure, extractive reserves are not a panacea; they are still vulnerable to extensive depredations by illegal loggers, ranchers, and farmers, for instance, and the legal extractivists often fail to make steady profits, particularly now that they are partly at the mercy of unpredictable international markets. But the reserves unquestionably hold great potential as models of sustainable development. Moreover, they prove the value of linking the environmental and human rights policy agendas: neither movement could have accomplished anything nearly as effective on its own.

## Individuals: The Traditional Human Rights Focus

"You can't reason with eco-freaks, but you can sure scare them."

> — Rick Sieman, director of the Sahara Club, an anti-environmental organization whose newsletter lists environmentalists' names, addresses, phone numbers, and license plates[30]

Perhaps the most graphic illustrations of the need for human rights workers and environmentalists to join forces are the abuses endured by individual activists—whose only crimes, in general, have been organizing protests and speaking their minds. This is the traditional realm of the human rights movement: by focusing on individualized cases, the movement's representatives have effectively demonstrated that no grassroots campaign can be successful if the basic rights of the individual are not respected, that civil liberties are the most important check on a government's power. They have also found that publicizing the plight of individuals can be a particularly effective way of exposing abuses of power and making them tangible to the general public.

When traditional human rights stories—involving the harassment or torture or imprisonment or murder of activists—do penetrate the mass media, though, they too often come across as tragic but isolated instances of criminal activities. What environmentalists have added to this realm of advocacy is an awareness of the broader trends driving many of these acts of violence. Certainly, the basic issue is usually one of personal safety and law enforcement. But often behind these examples of brutality are long-standing struggles over environmental justice.[31]

Tragically, the list of atrocities committed against environmental activists is quite long, and global in reach. (See Table 1.) Over the past year, for example, drug barons and loggers in Mexico have murdered dozens of Tarahumara Indians fighting to preserve the remote forests that make up their traditional homeland. A few environmentalists trying to aid in the struggle have also been killed, some apparently after being tortured. In Honduras, in February 1995, activist Blanca Jeannette Kawas Fernandez was assassinated by an unidentified man who simply walked up to her living room window and shot her. Kawas was the president of PROLANSATE, an environmental organization fighting illegal logging and government-backed development in Punta Sal National Park. Other Honduran activists suspect that her murderer is receiving government protection. Similarly, in Cambodia, journalist Chan Dara was found dead on December 8, 1994, two days after being warned by the military police to stop looking into the military's illegal involvement in the country's timber industry. Violence may also be brewing in northern Russia, where in October 1995 Secret Service officers confiscated computers, papers, photographs, and videos from a group of environmentalists trying to document the government's handling of radioactive waste

---

**TABLE 1**

# Attacks Against Environmental Activists, Selected Examples

| Activist and Affiliation | Attack |
| --- | --- |
| Piotr Kozhevnikov, government water inspector, former Soviet Union | Kozhevnikov was arrested and placed in a psychiatric ward as punishment for trying to publicize illegal government dumping of oil and sludge into the Gulf of Finland in 1986. |
| Barbara D'Achille, environmental journalist, Peru | D'Achille was murdered on May 31, 1989, by Shining Path guerrillas, in retaliation for the journalist's exposés of the impact of coca cultivation on the rain forest. |
| Henry Domoldol, Isneg tribal leader, Philippines | Domoldol was murdered on June 26, 1991, by members of a militia with ties to the Philippine Army; Domoldol had publicized military involvement in illegal logging of local tribal lands. |
| Mahesh Chandra Mehta, General Secretary, Indian Council for Enviro-Legal Action, India | Mehta, an environmental lawyer whose petitions have shut down some 2,000 dirty industrial operations in India, faces death threats regularly and has at times been pressured by large gangs of hired thugs to drop his cases. |
| Guy Pence, Forest Service ranger, United States | Pence was the target of two bomb attacks in 1995 but escaped unharmed; he has been outspoken on the issue of enforcing federal grazing regulations. |

*Source*: Compiled by Worldwatch Institute from sources cited in endnote 32.

---

problems.[32]

Other abuses arise from conflicts over the development of resources right in the heart of cities, rather than in frontier areas. In March 1992, Nairobi police assaulted a group of Kenyan women who were peacefully protesting the imprisonment of several environmentalists and the construction of a 62-story office building in a downtown park. The group's leader, Professor Wangari Maathai, an internationally acclaimed activist who started Kenya's Green Belt Movement to plant trees and work for gender equality, was beaten unconscious and then arrested. Just one month earlier, in Acapulco, Mexico, Dr. Javier Mojica, the leader of an environmental campaign protesting the construction of a shopping mall in the city's only park, was beaten severely in his own home. Local police, who activists believe were involved in the crime, have passed off the assailants as common thieves and neglected to conduct a thorough investigation. In September 1995, a bomb went off in the offices of a Greek environmental organization in a small coastal city just a few hours after a local politician had announced that he wouldn't mind "throwing all ecologists out of [town]." The environmentalists, one of whom was wounded in the blast, had been lobbying peacefully for more restrictions on tourist development and for the creation of a marine park to protect the nesting habitat of an endangered sea turtle.[33]

In countries like the United States, with strong human rights laws and a free press, abuses tend to be less institutional in nature but no less widespread. Journalist David Helvarg recently filled an entire book with documented cases of anti-green violence in the United States. American environmentalists have been the victims of vandalism, harassment, assaults, and even torture, rape, arson, and murder. Pat Costner, Greenpeace USA's toxics coordinator, watched her house mysteriously burn to the ground just a few weeks before her report criticizing hazardous waste incinerators was scheduled to be published. Investigators later found the fuel can arsonists had used to express their support of incineration. In Oregon, two local environmental activists were lynched in effigy one day before a conference hosted by Ron Arnold, the founder of the "Wise Use" movement, which lobbies for expanded logging, ranching, and mining rights and the abolition of all environmental legislation. The tarred and feathered effigies held a sign that read, "Enviros can learn a lot from a couple of dummies."[34]

Some Wise Users actually take pride in claiming responsibility for the harassment of environmental activists in the United States. They say that no government agent or grassroots organizer should be allowed to interfere with how a given landowner wants to use or abuse natural resources—and they will go to great lengths to thwart such "interference." Many members of Wise Use also belong to the so-called Counties Movement, which pressures county sheriffs to arrest federal land managers who do not allow loggers, miners, and ranchers their unofficial but time-honored privilege of extracting resources from public lands without limit.[35]

In trying to present themselves as victims, Wise Users and their allies have argued that environmental concepts, which tend to be concerned with the well-being of society as a whole, pose a direct threat to the individual liberties that are so central to the American tradition. One study by the Cato Institute, for instance, asserted that pollution-monitoring regulations subject property owners to unwarranted searches and deprive them of their right not to incriminate themselves. But U.S. legislation has endorsed the notion that the right of downstream communities to be free from pollution supersedes the right of property owners to be free from environmental monitoring. Wise Users want rights to come with none of the usual accompanying responsibilities, with no recognition of mutual dependence—with no strings attached at all.[36]

Public efforts to recognize the work of individual activists have been particularly helpful in distinguishing the rights-based approach of environmental justice campaigns from the distortions of the Wise Use people. Frequently, even limited investigative journalism makes it clear who the victims are and who the abusers of power are. And committees responsible for awarding official prizes often conduct extensive investigations to document the relevant environmental injustices and human rights abuses—which often occur in remote areas under obscured conditions.[37]

Every December, the Swedish Parliament holds a press conference on the day before the Nobel Prizes are presented and gives out its Right Livelihood Award—known widely as the "Alternative Nobel Prize"—to leaders of self-help movements around the world. And every spring the San Francisco-based Goldman Foundation awards its prestigious Environmental Prize to one grassroots activist from each of the six continents. Newspaper articles inspired by the Goldman award ceremonies and videos produced by the foundation itself bring environmental justice struggles home to a wide audience. Many of the Goldman winners come from communities directly threatened by development projects or toxic dumps, and many have been unjustly imprisoned or otherwise abused because of their activism. Their stories help the public understand what is at stake at the most personal level, understand that human rights abuses are not just isolated crimes and that environmentalism is not just about the rights of nature.[38]

## Communities: Local People Fighting for Their Environments

"All socioeconomic groupings tend to resent the nearby siting of major facilities, but middle and upper socioeconomic strata possess better resources to effectuate their opposition. Middle and higher socioeconomic strata neighborhoods should not fall within the one-mile and five-mile radius of the proposed site."

> — *Cerrell Associates, consultants to the California Waste Management Board, explaining that it is easiest to build incinerators in low-income neighborhoods with a high percentage of non-voters, in their 1984 report, "Political Difficulties Facing Waste-to-Energy Conversion Plant Siting"*[39]

Perhaps the most significant result of publicity campaigns on behalf of individual activists is the revelation of their broader struggles for environmental justice—whether on behalf of an ethnic minority, an indigenous community, a particular group of marginalized women, or simply people without the resources to secure a home and livelihood. International law guards individual and national sovereignty, but communities and other small groups often find themselves caught in a kind of no-man's land, fighting a mining installation or government-sponsored toxic dump with no official legal protection.[40]

In the industrial world, community-level environmental struggles are often against the pollution generated by large companies. The companies' public relations people tend to pass off their toxic emissions as unfortunate but necessary byproducts of their efforts to provide crucial services for customers—or even, in the case of defense contractors, for the sake of national security. In the developing world, the issue at hand is almost always one of "national development": activists end up fighting projects that seem unduly disruptive on a human level and unsustainable on an ecological level but that are being pushed by the government as engines of economic growth. Officials often argue that the proposed dam or power plant or tourist resort would benefit most of the country's citizens directly—through jobs or access to water or electricity—and would also earn foreign exchange. But all too often, no matter what the government's intentions, most of the benefits go to wealthy elites and most of the costs are borne by marginalized communities.[41]

The Ogoni people of southern Nigeria are one such community, threatened by the oil-drilling projects of the Shell Petroleum Development Company and fighting not just for environmental justice but for their very survival. Marginal communities become even more vulnerable under rights-repressive regimes like the one currently ruling Nigeria, and the plight of the Ogoni was dramatic enough to spur major collaborative efforts among international human rights and environmental organizations. Much of the publicity and advocacy surrounding the situation in Ogoniland came in response to the eloquent appeals of Ken Saro-Wiwa, the president of the Movement for the Survival of Ogoni People (MOSOP) and a nominee for the Nobel Peace Prize. Saro-Wiwa received the Right Livelihood Award in December 1994, and the Goldman Environmental Prize the next spring. But on November 10, 1995, he and eight other MOSOP leaders were executed by Nigeria's illegitimate military regime in retaliation for their activism—and in defiance of international protests. The Ogoni, meanwhile, besides having to absorb this tragic injustice, still face the daunting task of saving their homeland from the local environmental ravages of our global dependence on oil.[42]

Initially, the situation in Ogoniland seemed to be just one among many instances of systematic human rights abuse perpetrated under the auspices of the Nigerian military dictatorship. Since May 1994, the 1,050-square-kilometer region, home to 500,000 Ogoni, a minority people who make up just one-half of one percent of Nigeria's population, has also housed an immense military police force, with members drawn from the Nigerian Army, Navy, and Air Force. According to "Operation Order No. 4/94—Restoration of Law and Order in Ogoniland," the police force had been installed in order to "ensure that...non-indigenous residents carrying out business ventures...within Ogoniland are not molested." The only non-indigenous business people in Ogoniland are employees of Shell, which accounts for 50 percent of Nigeria's crude oil output. Oil profits provide 90 percent of Nigeria's foreign exchange and 80 percent of government revenue.[43]

MOSOP was founded in 1992 specifically to campaign against what it refers to as Shell's reign of "environmental terrorism." The once lush agricultural land of the Niger Delta is now covered in oil slicks that stretch for kilometers; vegetation has died and some rivers run black; gas flares near villages poison the air and cause acid rain; and unlined toxic waste pits allow pollution to seep into drinking water supplies. The "molestation" and disruptions of law and order referred to by the police edict have consisted largely of peaceful demonstrations staged by MOSOP. The Ogoni farmers and fishers have simply demanded that Shell do ecological and social impact studies of their oil extraction operations and provide compensation for the damage that has already been done.[44]

Even before the military occupation order, the police had defied international law and committed gross human rights violations against the Ogoni people, seizing the passports of MOSOP leaders when they tried to meet with other human rights workers overseas, firing into crowds at peaceful demonstrations, and organizing outright attacks against small villages. Oil company representatives, meanwhile, accept no responsibility whatsoever for the government's violent tactics. But one public affairs official did acknowledge that Shell has often asked the military regime for assistance with Ogoni demonstrators, explaining that the company "has a legal obligation to notify authorities whenever it perceives a threat to the continuity of oil operations." Shell also denies charges that it has devastated the Ogoni's environment. Banking on the government's complicity, though, the company has never done any environmental assessments before digging wells or laying pipes. Of the total number of spills recorded over the past decade in the 100 or so countries where Shell operates, 40 percent occurred in Nigeria.[45]

The sacrificing of small communities like those in Ogoniland is, unfortunately, a common phenomenon around the globe. (See Table 2.) Such abuses occur with regularity even under rights-protective regimes. The U.S. environmental justice movement first crystallized, in fact, in response to a government-backed scheme to use a particularly vulnerable community as a dumping ground for hazardous materials. In the fall of 1982, the state of North Carolina applied to the U.S. Environmental Protection Agency (EPA) for a permit to dump 29,000 metric tons of soil contaminated with polychlorinated biphenyls (PCBs)—the chemical that made Love Canal famous—in the impoverished town of Afton, whose population is 84 percent

**TABLE 2**

# Community-level Environmental Injustices, Selected Examples

| Community | Problem |
|---|---|
| Udege indigenous people, Siberia, Russia | Logging by Russian, Japanese, South Korean, and U.S. firms has destroyed the Udege's resource base and caused severe soil erosion and siltation of river systems. |
| Mining communities, Wales, United Kingdom | Government encouragement of open-cast coal mining has resulted in water pollution and increased instances of pulmonary disease in Welsh communities. |
| Yami indigenous people, Orchid Island, Taiwan | For 13 years, the Taiwanese government has stored nuclear waste on Orchid Island, in metal drums now beginning to rust. In the mid-seventies, the government had told the Yami, who lack formal education, that the storage facility they were building would be a fish cannery. |
| Amazonian Indians, Oriente region, Ecuador | Oil exploitation has devastated the environments of several indigenous groups, leaving water supplies with ten to a thousand times the level of contamination allowable in the U.S. |
| Village fisherfolk, Mdulumanja, Malawi | In 1991, the owner of a hotel on Lake Malawi received government permission to evict an entire community for the sake of tourist development, bulldozing more than 70 homes and offering no relocation plan. |

*Source*: Compiled by Worldwatch Institute from sources cited in endnote 46.

African-American. EPA granted its approval, even though its own regulations clearly ruled Afton out as a possible site for PCB disposal. Standard EPA guidelines require a buffer zone of at least 50 feet between the ground surface and the underground water table. In Afton, the underground water table is a mere 10 to 15 feet below the surface, and most of the town's residents draw their water from local wells.[46]

Native Americans have also been particularly hard hit by environmental injustices in the United States. Western tribes, for instance, have had to shoulder a disproportionate share of the cost incurred by the government's exploitation of national uranium supplies. Approximately 65 percent of North America's uranium deposits lie inside Native American reservations. But those reservations have been home to 80 percent of the uranium mining done in the United States and 100 percent of the processing, largely because reservations fall outside the jurisdiction of most state and federal environmental laws and reservation residents have no authority to make their own protective regulations.[47]

With such large reserves of the valuable ore, and given the federal government's historical commitment to nuclear development, many Native American communities should by now have become quite wealthy. Thanks largely to federal land managers, though, whose main goal was to provide preferred companies with the cheapest possible exploitation rights, Native Americans have tended to receive as little as 3.4 percent of the market value for uranium extracted from their lands. Native Americans also have the lowest per capita income of any demographic group in America and the highest per capita rates of malnutrition, disease, and infant mortality.[48]

The Navajo community in particular has suffered from cancers, respiratory ailments, miscarriages, and birth defects caused by radiation. In almost all cases, the people who worked in the mines never received protective clothing or medical checkups or even basic information about the risks of exposure to uranium, and virtually no victims have ever gained any type of compensation. To this day, many Native American communities have to live with illegally high levels of lead, thorium, and radium, among other toxins that have seeped into their water and soil from tailings ponds and processing plants.[49]

Other community-level environmental injustices stem directly from government-sponsored infrastructure projects—many of which are promoted as beneficial for local peoples. In China, for instance, government officials have touted the construction of the Three Gorges Dam—intended to be the largest hydroelectric project in the world—as providing much-improved flood control and navigation for downstream communities. But most of the dam's massive electricity-generating capabilities will serve the Shanghai metropolitan area, hundreds of kilometers to the east. And several teams of engineers have asserted that building the dam will in fact increase the danger of local flooding and make navigation more difficult.[50]

**Of the last decade's spills in the 100 or so countries where Shell operates, 40 percent occurred in Nigeria.**

At the very least, the construction of the dam will flood about 20 towns and 11,000 hectares of farmland, threaten several endangered species such as the Siberian white crane and the White Flag dolphin, and uproot some 1.4 million people—nearly equivalent to the current population of Kuwait. Most of these displaced persons will end up on much higher ground, with colder, poorer soils. A study by the Chinese Academy of Sciences acknowledged that five times as much new land would be necessary to equal crop yields in the fertile valley fields that will soon be below the dam's reservoir. Nevertheless, in December 1994, Chinese Premier Li Peng poured the first of the concrete to inaugurate the 14-year dam-building process, shunting aside warnings from scores of international experts that the location of the dam makes it particularly vulnerable to earthquakes and landslides and that silt accumulation in the reservoir will shrink its capacity significantly within just a few years.[51]

Within China, in the years leading up to the decision to break ground on the project, the government systematically suppressed information and opinions questioning the viability of the dam. Police arrested several protesters, including the environmental journalist Dai Qing, who in 1989 edited the first Chinese book criticizing the dam, *Yangtze! Yangtze!* And the government made no effort to consult with local people about the dam's impact or to provide them with legal channels to appeal their compensation. Human Rights Watch has suggested that "the true function of the Three Gorges Dam [may] simply be to stand...as an ultimate symbol of the power and authority of the state."[52]

Sometimes a large infrastructure project like a dam might truly serve the common good—but only when a serious effort has been made to analyze and mitigate the consequences for all affected parties. More often, as the above examples demonstrate, nations and corporations choose to facilitate their planning process by treating certain small communities as expendable. Just within the past decade, infrastructure projects involving general urban development as well as road and dam construction have displaced an estimated 80 to 90 million people globally.[53]

**Within the past decade, large infrastructure projects have displaced an estimated 80 to 90 million people globally.**

When communal rights receive the respect they deserve, however, communities often turn out to be ideal promoters of sustainability. While large infrastructure or extraction projects are often inherently destructive to surrounding ecosystems, smaller-scale projects can usually be made to work in harmony with the local landscape. And if the project is small enough that community members can administer it, it is much more likely to be welcomed and accepted.

In recent years, community-based conservation and development schemes have become much more common—thanks to local initiatives sponsored both by the communities themselves and by teams of environmentalists and human rights workers who have recognized that sustainability must encompass both ecology and social justice, as well as economic viability. (See Table 3.)[54]

In Costa Rica, for instance, 12 peasant farmers came together in 1988 to form the San Miguel Association for Conservation and Development (ASACODE), in an attempt to keep local forests under the control of local communities. Some 27 percent of Costa Rica's land falls within some sort of preserve, yet the country has Central America's highest rate of deforestation, because the timber industry, which accounts for 90 percent of forest destruction nationwide, has been systematically buying out small landowners in forested regions like San Miguel. ASACODE provides incentives to local people to hold onto their land by showing them ways of harvesting and processing wood sustainably, without harming the forest, and has worked to develop regional markets for artisanal wood products.[55]

**When communal rights are respected, communities often turn out to be ideal promoters of sustainability.**

More and more local people have been reneging on deals with large timber companies in favor of joining ASACODE, because ASACODE's efficient use of wood and targeted marketing have generated immediate profits. Industrial timber operations, which waste up to half of each tree they cut, often insist on paying landowners very low prices for logging rights. Moreover, ASACODE's ecologically sound harvesting techniques leave much more of the forest intact for long-term use. And ASACODE has further encouraged community stability and stewardship by using its profits to start group-managed tree nurseries for native species and to organize study sessions for neighboring villagers.[56]

**TABLE 3**

# Community-based Conservation and Development Initiatives, Selected Examples

| Community/Organization | Initiative |
| --- | --- |
| *Sangam* project, Deccan Development Society (DDS), Andhra Pradesh, India | DDS helps organize *sangams*, communities of women, in southern Indian villages, to work toward gender equity, establish credit programs, cultivate and use medicinal herbs, incorporate organic farming techniques and multi-cropping systems into agricultural practices, and plant trees. |
| Yanesha Forestry Cooperative (COFYAL), Peruvian Amazon | COFYAL is a sustainable forestry co-op run by the Yanesha Indians, who earn a living exporting forest products to Europe and the United States, while also protecting the rain forest from clear-cutting by ranchers and developers. |
| Association for the Protection of the Environment (APE), Cairo, Egypt | APE coordinates the efforts of Cairo's trashpickers, who earn a living by recycling paper, using organic wastes as fertilizer, and weaving rugs from discarded scraps of cotton. |
| InterTribal Sinkyone Wilderness Council (ITSWC), northern California | In early 1995, the ten tribes of the ITSWC won back some 1,600 hectares of ancestral redwood rain forest from the state of California. Their plan is to create a wilderness park—complete with four traditional villages—that will serve as a model for sustainable land use. |

| | |
|---|---|
| Annapurna Conservation Area Project (ACAP), central Nepal | ACAP has made local participation the cornerstone of its efforts to increase the direct benefits of tourism while decreasing its environmental impact—by improving local lodging services, using kerosene instead of trees for fuel, and enforcing a Minimum Impact Code for trekkers. |
| Kakadu National Park, northern Australia | Kakadu is co-managed by the government's park service and the aborigines who have inhabited the region for more than 50,000 years. Co-management has fostered effective nature conservation, a tourist industry that provides the aborigines with a steady income, and the preservation of traditional communities. |

*Source:* Compiled by Worldwatch Institute from sources cited in endnote 54.

Communities will be an integral part of any sustainable development schemes that succeed over the long term. Of course, some large infrastructure projects, sponsored by both the public and private sectors, continue to be necessary, especially in major cities. Programs facilitating the transfer of clean energy technologies from northern to southern countries, for instance, have immense potential even if their scope ends up extending far beyond community control. Investments in sewage treatment plants or rail lines could also yield high returns. But most environmentally sound development projects will probably come out of community-level initiatives that provide local people with relevant ecological information and empower them to take more control of their own fate. Policymakers could bring us all closer to sustainability by focusing on ways to give local people a stake in preserving their immediate environments.[57]

## Countries: Injustices Across Borders

"States have...the sovereign right to exploit their own resources pursuant to their own environmental policies, and the responsibility to ensure that activities within their own jurisdiction or control do not cause damage to the environment of other States or of areas beyond the limits of national jurisdiction."

> —*Principle 21, Declaration of the U.N.*
> *Conference on the Human Environment,*
> *Stockholm, June 1972*[58]

Despite the centrality of communities, some environmental justice issues extend far beyond the local level. A considerable amount of pollution crosses borders, for instance, as do rivers and environmental refugees. Many environmental resources are in fact shared by everyone— oceans, forests, genetic diversity, climate, the ozone layer— and thus form a kind of global commons. And the people responsible for the degradation of the global commons are not always the ones who suffer the consequences. The Antarctic ozone hole, for instance, which has resulted in increasing skin cancer rates in the South, was caused largely by chlorofluorocarbon (CFC) emissions in the North. No community or even country, meanwhile, can singlehandedly protect the oceans sufficiently to ensure sustainable yields from salt-water fisheries, or cut carbon emissions enough to curtail the disruptions in weather caused by global climate change. Such global threats require not just activists from different movements but entire countries to work together.[59]

The United Nations has considerable potential as a binding force to help mount global conservation campaigns. It was founded on the premise of international interdependence, after all, in the wake of World War II. Yet the founding nations were careful to protect their national sovereignty. What one country did with its natural resources, for instance, was nobody else's business. One of the U.N.'s most crucial roles in the future, however, may be mediating between one country's alleged right to burn down its forests and another country's alleged right to burn fossil fuels—and perhaps yet another country's alleged right to block both of the other entitlements.[60]

Every person on earth depends on a stable climate and an intact ozone layer and clean air and water and healthy oceans. Yet the elite wealthy classes, in both the industrial and developing worlds, tend to contribute more to most types of environmental degradation than any other group of people. And the poorer classes tend to pay more of the costs of ecological damage.[61]

This divide is especially pronounced between the North and South. Though the North is not devoid of poverty and the South does not lack a class of elites, average levels of resource consumption are far higher in industrial countries than in developing countries. People living in the industrial world comprise only about 21 percent of the global population, and that share is decreasing, given the faster rate of population growth in the developing world. But industrial countries consume about 86 percent of the globe's aluminum, 81 percent of its paper, 80 percent of its iron and steel, 75 percent of its energy, and 61 percent of its meat. Consequently, they are responsible for the vast majority of the hazardous wastes created by the mining and smelting of aluminum and iron ores, the clearcutting of forests for the sake of paper production, the air pollution and build-up of greenhouse gases caused by fossil-fuel burning, and the soil erosion on grazing lands.[62]

Many of these degrading activities, though, occur disproportionately in developing countries: just as in colonial times, many poor nations end up despoiling their own lands in order to export certain products that feed the richer nations' habit of overconsumption—and also to provide their own elites with steady profits. While developing nations account for only 18 percent of global copper consumption, for instance, they produce about 47 percent of what the world uses. Moreover, because extractive technologies in such countries tend to be less advanced than those in the North, and because there is often little enforcement of legal safeguards against pollution, the environmental toll in copper-producing countries of the South—the release of heavy metals and chemical contaminants in local soils and water supplies, for instance—tends to be even worse than the production statistics might imply.[63]

The international trade in toxic substances provides a particularly good illustration of these disparities. Industrial countries are responsible for more than 90 percent of the 360 million metric tons of hazardous waste produced globally each year: inherently unsustainable industrial practices in the richer countries are directly responsible for almost all of the world's incinerator ash, dioxin, and PCBs. It is almost impossible to keep track of what happens to those wastes, but experts believe that at least 30 million metric tons a year cross national borders, with a high percentage going to poorer countries. Over the last five years, there have been at least 299 documented dumpings in Eastern Europe, 239 in Asia, 148 in Latin America, and 30 in Africa.[64]

In many cases, increased waste shipments from industrial nations have been an unintended consequence of the tightening of domestic dumping regulations: in the late 1980s, largely because of new laws, hazardous waste disposal prices climbed to about $275 per metric ton in the United States. In Africa, meanwhile, where environmental regulations—and appropriate disposal technologies—were virtually non-existent, the per-ton price was often as low as $2.75. Many African countries were willing to accept the toxic shipments because they were accompanied by much-needed foreign exchange. Of course, in many cases, the incoming money doesn't get beyond the particular government officials or businessmen who worked out the import deal; but much of the country ends up paying the costs of disposing of the toxic materials.[65]

At times, importing countries do not even realize exactly what they are receiving. In 1987, for instance, Jamaica accepted a shipment of milk powder from Europe under the label "humanitarian assistance"; the powder turned out to be contaminated with radioactive wastes from the Chernobyl disaster. In 1988, an Italian waste company offered a Nigerian farmer $100 a month to use his backyard as a storage area for 8,000 barrels of "fertilizer." When the leaky barrels burst open in the sun, they turned out to be filled with industrial wastes containing asbestos fibers and high levels of PCBs, and much of the community ended up with health problems and a contaminated water supply. In 1992, several U.S. firms collaborated to mix in about 900 metric tons of toxic copper-smelter furnace dust with fertilizer being shipped to the government of Bangladesh. Several Bangladeshi farmers had spread the poisonous fertilizer on their crops before the scandal became public.[66]

**Industrial countries are responsible for more than 90 percent of the 360 million metric tons of hazardous waste produced globally each year.**

Over the past few years, various international policymakers, working closely with environmental and social justice activists, have produced some treaties that could help protect the developing world from some of this pollution. The U.N.'s Basel Convention of 1992, for instance, a document for which Greenpeace in particular lobbied tirelessly, requires exporters of hazardous wastes to gain fully informed consent from importers prior to any transaction, and mandates that exporters take responsibility for ensuring that importers can dispose of the wastes in an ecologically sound manner. More importantly, in 1994, all the parties to the Convention agreed to a general ban on the export of toxic wastes. Several significant countries, though, including the United States, which generates about 85 percent of the world's hazardous discards, still had not even ratified the original convention. And the ban on cross-border toxic trading, if not backed by a production ban, could end up just encouraging the dirtiest industries simply to relocate to the developing world.[67]

This migratory trend is in fact already under way. U.S. companies, for instance, have sent more than 2,000 factories across the Mexican border—the infamous *maquiladoras*—where according to liberal trade rules they receive duty-free imports of parts which they then process into products to be exported back into the United States. Mexican workers at the *maquiladoras* earn a fraction of what Americans would get for comparable labor, and they live among free-flowing streams of toxic chemicals. Though Mexican environmental laws are relatively strict, enforcement is minimal. A survey of six *maquiladoras* by the U.S. General Accounting Office (GAO) revealed that none had acquired the environmental permit required by Mexican law. Under a 1983 agreement between the two countries, waste from the *maquiladoras* must be returned to the United States for disposal. As of the early 1990s, though, only about two to three percent of the firms bound by this pact were actually complying with it.[68]

Meanwhile, despite the gradual tightening of regulations governing exports of hazardous wastes, world trade in general is being freed by pacts like the North American Free Trade Agreement (NAFTA) and the General Agreement on Tariffs and Trade (GATT). Some kinds of trade can help protect the environment by forcing out dirty, inefficient industries and by promoting the transfer of clean technologies. But free trade has also broadened the dissemination of dangerous products, such as pesticides.[69]

Agrochemical companies now target developing-world markets even more than in the past, and have had increasing success there selling pesticides that are banned in the industrial world—just as cigarette companies now generate some of their biggest profits in developing countries where there is less public awareness of nicotine's health effects. The developing world currently accounts for just 19 percent of total pesticide consumption. Yet studies suggest that about half of all pesticide poisonings and 80 percent of all verifiable pesticide-related deaths occur in the poorer nations—because many developing governments still have not put restrictions on toxicity levels.[70]

Even when governments of poor nations have banned certain chemicals, manufacturers have sometimes challenged them in court, and, by invoking free-trade law, have won back their right to import and sell their products. In 1991, for instance, the multinational chemical company Hoechst overturned the Philippine government's ban on one of their key products, the pesticide endosulfan. As of 1989, the GAO estimated that about a quarter of the pesticides the U.S. was sending abroad were banned domestically; ironically, many of them return home on imported fruit. A 1990 study, meanwhile, argued that the number of developing-world agricultural workers being poisoned each year could be as high as 25 million—equivalent to the entire population of Peru. In 1993, the U.N.'s Food and Agriculture Organiza-tion (FAO) surveyed various nations to determine compliance with its International Code of Conduct on the Distribution and Use of Pesticides. In 83 percent of the developing-world case studies the FAO conducted, researchers found that farmers and farmworkers received virtually no training material relating to pesticide application.[71]

**In 83 percent of the developing-world case studies, farmers received no training material relating to pesticide application.**

A key factor in the poorer countries' willingness to use highly toxic pesticides and even occasionally accept deadly hazardous waste shipments is their lingering debt crisis. Most pesticide use in the developing world goes not toward domestic food production but toward cash crops grown for export to richer countries. During the Ethiopian famine of 1983-84, while people died of hunger, fields just a few kilometers away bloomed with carefully cultivated, pest-free carnations. Often, poor countries take this route specifically at the behest of richer countries or multilateral donor institutions like the World Bank and the International Monetary Fund (IMF). The need of many developing countries to earn foreign exchange is undeniable, but too often income-generating projects have come at the expense of both social safety nets and the environment.[72]

Pressure to adopt environmentally destructive practices, in particular, is rampant, and comes not just from the North but also from other southern countries. Three large timber conglomerates from Indonesia and Malaysia, for instance, have offered the cash-starved government of Suriname a multi-million-dollar deal for the logging rights to a 2.8-million-hectare tract of rain forest—an area that encompasses more than a quarter of the small South American country. Desperate to sustain their businesses as tree stocks shrink back home, the Asian companies have allegedly gone so far as to bribe several of the parliamentarians who will be voting on the proposal. One firm apparently garnered the support of Surinamese foreign minister Subhaas Mungra by appointing his brother to be the head of its local operations.[73]

Despite the undeniable infusion of cash and new jobs the companies would provide by investing in Suriname's economy, the deal is patently unfair, with the firms offering approximately one-tenth the per-hectare market value for logging rights and giving out a royalty of less than 7 percent. While the logging companies are projected to make about $28 million a year over the next 25 years, Suriname is likely to get just $2 million annually. Moreover, the proposal completely ignores Suriname's long-term prospects from both an economic and an ecological standpoint, making no provisions for reforestation or any other environmental easement strategies, or even for monitoring of the damage. In addition, the logging as currently planned would decimate the homelands of three groups of indigenous forest dwellers.[74]

The Surinamese people, like the *pepineros* on the Galápagos or any other community, have the right to control their own destiny, and sacrificing part of the country's rain forest may eventually become an economic necessity. But Surinamese decision makers also have a responsibility to the country's indigenous peoples and to the international community. Selling off the forest to outside logging companies who have no incentive to protect the environment or Suriname's long-term prospects would seem to serve the best interests of just a few people: an elite group of government officials in Suriname and an elite group of business executives in Indonesia and Malaysia.

Recognizing the extent to which we all depend on the services that forests provide, the international community has proposed alternative schemes that could both prop up Suriname's economy and preserve its ecological treasures. Early in 1995, Enrique V. Iglesias, president of the Inter-American Development Bank (IDB), sent a letter to Suriname president Ronald Venetiaan promising a significant aid package if the country blocked or at least postponed the logging deal. The IDB money would go toward training forestry professionals and launching an ecotourism industry within the nation's already extensive network of wildlife preserves. Iglesias's offer reinforced the value of a strategy human rights workers have advocated for years: both multilateral and bilateral lenders can use their financial leverage to encourage better governance, perhaps by cutting off aid if a government has become repressive, or, more constructively, by earmarking funds for sustainable development projects, especially those that protect basic civil liberties.[75]

**During the Ethiopian famine of 1983-84, while people died of hunger, fields bloomed with carefully cultivated, pest-free carnations.**

Foreign diplomats and international environmentalists have also contributed sustainable development plans to Suriname. Besides backing Iglesias's nature-based tourism suggestion, the proposals recommend expanding a fledgling project that brings together ethnobotanical researchers from around the world with local medicine men to search for marketable drugs. Such rain forest pharmaceuticals have occasionally brought huge profits; in this case, the money would be shared equitably among the local community members, the country as a whole, and any pharmaceutical company involved.[76]

Cross-border environmental justice issues involving the global commons—and necessitating coordinated international action—are plentiful. Threats to cropland, oceanic fisheries, and the protective ozone layer are all serious. But the most overarching global problem we now face is the prospect of climate change. Global warming will affect everyone. But it is an environmental justice issue both because the northern countries played a much larger role than the southern countries in spurring it, and because the South will likely have a much harder time than the North dealing with its consequences.

Currently, the industrial countries are responsible for about 70 percent of global emissions of carbon, the main contributor to greenhouse gases. Per-capita carbon emissions in the United States are about 20 times higher than in India. And people living in India and most other developing nations will be especially hard hit by global warming because their regional climate is already quite hot, making them highly susceptible to drought and desertification. Small island states, meanwhile, and the developing world's coastal nations, will have to face a rise in the level of the oceans with hardly any dependable infrastructure in place to deal with flooding. For developing nations in particular, the greenhouse effect could mean a crippling loss of cropland, the creation of millions of environmental refugees, and an expansion in the range of tropical diseases.[77]

In attempting to address such problems, which have so overwhelmingly broad a scope, the human rights approach—with its roots firmly planted in local activism—might seem out of place. Slowing global warming will necessitate action on the most wide-ranging international level, and will entail the reform of the energy industry in the richer countries, the transfer of clean technologies to the poorer countries, and the reforestation of areas all around the world. Yet one of the keys to reaching even these broadest of goals is without doubt the protection of basic human rights.

Especially because global warming is a justice issue—because some countries are more vulnerable and have more at stake than others—there need to be firm measures in place to hold entire nations and industries accountable for their actions, to ensure that all parties are contributing their fair share to what has to be a universal effort. Scientists, government officials, representatives of non-governmental organizations, and private citizen activists, whether from the United States or India, all ought to have a voice in determining how to cope with climate change.

Indeed, at the U.N.'s Berlin Conference of the Parties to the Rio Climate Treaty, held in April 1995, outspoken advocacy by the well-organized Alliance of Small Island States (AOSIS)—demanding equal protection for the people most vulnerable to climate change—played a key role in the negotiations. For the first time, the developing world took the lead in pursuing measures to slow global warming. Diplomats at Berlin hammered out agreements to begin significant transfers of clean technologies from North to South and, within a few years, to force the most carbon-intensive countries not just to stabilize but to reduce their emissions.[78]

Of course, any U.N. treaty or other international agreement can have an impact beyond the level of abstraction only if all countries make monitoring and enforcement their highest priority. This in turn requires rights-protective regimes and citizens who recognize their civic duty and are both willing and able to take an active role in their community. People need to have full access to information about a particular country's or company's carbon emissions and to be able to spread that information in the international media and demand compliance with international standards. Moreover, as the Berlin meeting indicated, one of the best ways to spur the adoption of meaningful treaties in the first place is through the active exercising of civil liberties by well-informed, outspoken advocates.

The 1987 Montreal Protocol on Substances that Deplete the Ozone Layer was signed and implemented so quickly largely because of the activist role played by the international scientific community, international environmental organizations, and the chemical industry. In the United

States, environmentalists had already convinced policymakers to sign the world's strictest ozone legislation, which in turn had spurred leaders of American industry to become vocal supporters of international regulations that would allow them to compete on a level playing field in the global marketplace. The free exchange of information and ideas encouraged by the protection of basic rights, then, can lead to the recognition of common ground—sometimes even between environmentalists and industry groups—and subsequently to the building of coalitions. These in turn could potentially generate the political will necessary to move toward greater equity and sustainability at all levels of society.[79]

## The Human Rights Framework for Sustainable Development

"We have talked long enough... about equal rights.... It is time now to write the next chapter—and to write it in the books of law."

> — *Lyndon Baines Johnson, President of the United States, first address to Congress, November 27, 1963*[80]

Thanks to more than a decade of documenting problems, protesting, and building coalitions, environmentalists and human rights activists are now in a position to weave their combined agenda directly into official laws and policies. Taking a cue from the traditional human rights approach, they have mounted a strong effort to get the United Nations to set an official standard of environmental justice, to enshrine in international law every person's equal right to a healthy and healthful environment. Such a legal advance could be especially useful as a way of helping victims of environmental injustices to receive compensation. It might also eventually act as a preventive measure: if consistently backed up by swift, compensatory judicial enforcement, environmental human rights law could potentially force multinational corporations, for instance, to think twice about where and how they drill for oil.[81]

Perhaps even more important than establishing the substantive human rights relating to a healthy environment, however, will be a renewed emphasis on existing procedural rights. The actual prevention of environmental injustices will require not just strong laws and the threat of punishment from a strong judicial system, but also a drive to integrate basic civil liberties as explicitly as possible into sustainable development policies—locally, nationally, internationally, in corporations, and within institutions like the World Bank and the International Monetary Fund. If more development projects focused on encouraging environmental organizing, spurring local peoples' participation in key decisions, and providing access to environmental information, both the environment and the most vulnerable members of society would benefit substantially.[82]

The campaign to write environmental justice into international law is well under way, spearheaded by environmental lawyers and activists working in conjunction with the U.N.'s Sub-Commission on Prevention of Discrimination and Protection of Minorities. In 1989, a coalition of non-governmental organizations (NGOs) led by the Sierra Club Legal Defense Fund convinced the Sub-Commission to appoint a special rapporteur to make an international study of the overlap between human rights and environmental issues. The special rapporteur, Fatma Zohra Ksentini, issued her final report in August of 1994, documenting environmental injustices around the globe and pointing out the potential value of combining the ecological and human rights policy agendas. Just a few months before, a group of experts involved in the campaign had met in Geneva and issued the Draft Declaration of Principles on Human Rights and the Environment, which proclaimed, among other things, the universal human right to a "secure, healthy, ecologically sound environment." These two documents—supplemented by several international agreements dealing with sustainable development—are now serving as crucial tools in the effort to get the U.N.'s General Assembly to consider actually writing an official convention safeguarding environmental human rights.[83]

Although existing human rights conventions were written too early to reflect an awareness of environmental issues, many accepted rights have implicit environmental components. The International Covenant on Civil and Political Rights, for instance, guarantees the basic right to life, and the International Covenant on Economic, Social, and Cultural Rights guarantees the right to the highest attainable standard of health—both of which depend on a healthy environment. These and other well-established liberties, taken together with accepted ecological principles that have entered international law more recently, seem to indicate that there already exists an international moral consensus about each individual's right to freedom from environmental degradation. Thus the campaign to set a clearer legal standard of environmental justice is not so much demanding the recognition of a new set of substantive rights as ensuring that existing ones are fully protected, that nations follow through on commitments they've already made. Rather than detracting from traditional human rights advocacy, then, the fight for environmental justice should provide human rights activists with allies in the attempt to fulfill their mandate. Similarly, cooperation between the two movements should buttress environmentalists' efforts to implement the emerging body of international environmental law.[84]

To be sure, enforcement of international law remains a huge challenge. But one additional reason for couching environmental justice concerns in the language of human rights is that the international human rights system is more accessible than most other international law frameworks, making its treaties inherently more enforceable. They have a better chance than most international laws to act as deterrents, because under their auspices, individual victims of abuse can often bring a sovereign nation before an internationally recognized tribunal.[85]

In 1987, for instance, the Lubicon Lake Band of Indians in northern Canada, led by Bernard Ominayak, filed a complaint with the Human Rights Committee, the body established to deal with violations of the Covenant on Civil and Political Rights. Ominayak's petition asserted that state-sponsored oil and gas exploration was threatening the Indians' very means of subsistence and thus violating their right to life and to self-determination as a minority. Three years later, after a perhaps overly extensive investigation, the Committee upheld Ominayak's claim and upbraided the Canadian government before the international community. The state responded immediately by proposing to rectify the situation through measures to be deemed appropriate by the Committee. Though the U.N. process certainly labors under undue bureaucracy, there are times when it does eventually produce significant results.  Of course, national enforcement is still a concern: while the Lubicon Lake decision undeniably provides a powerful legal precedent, its practical significance for the Lubicon has so far been minimal, as the Band continues to face pressure from companies eager to capitalize on its resources.[86]

**There already exists an international moral consensus about each individual's right to freedom from environmental degradation.**

Environmental human rights mechanisms at the national and regional levels would also aid in the effort to establish substantive standards of environmental justice. Already, more than 60 national constitutions recognize at least some responsibility to protect the environment. The new government of South Africa, for example, adopted a constitution stipulating that "every person shall have the right to an environment which is not detrimental to his or her health or well-being." And both the European Court of Human Rights and the Inter-American Commission on Human Rights have recently tried cases involving environmental justice issues. Again, however, enforcement is the key. In Ecuador, the environmental laws on the books are both firm and explicit, but, as a former official of Petroecuador asserted in a 1994 affidavit, there is no effective enforcement apparatus to stop or remedy environmental pollution or natural resource depletion. Consequently, Texaco and other oil companies have conducted their operations in the Ecuadoran Amazon with virtually no government oversight, spilling hundreds of barrels of oil each week and despoiling the natural resource base of several indigenous groups. And a coalition of Quichua, Cofan, and Secoya Indians, together with some Amazonian colonists originally from other parts of Ecuador, had such difficulty getting the Ecuadoran courts to hear their environmental justice case that they ended up trying to sue Texaco in an American court.[87]

Perhaps the best way of preventing environmental injustices, meanwhile, would be development programs that explicitly foster the free exercise of people's basic civil liberties, the procedural rights whose very purpose is to facilitate the efforts of individuals and communities to safeguard their substantive rights. If a society has a large group of activist non-governmental organizations, a safe climate for protests, and a dynamic community of investigative journalists, then it can hold the government accountable when environmental and social policies turn out to be unsound or inequitable. The more community organizing that occurs, the broader the environmental justice coalition can become, and the more political power it can attain. Perhaps the most crucial human rights issue for sustainable development programs to focus on, then, is community participation.

Participatory projects are concrete, practical ways of applying the concept of self-determination, a right firmly established in the International Covenant on Civil and Political Rights and other instruments of international law. And the right to participation has been asserted in several other international documents, including Agenda 21, the program of action that came out of the U.N.'s 1992 Conference on Environment and Development held in Rio de Janeiro, and the Vienna Declaration from the U.N.'s 1993 Conference on Human Rights. In the past, development officers have tended simply to thrust their programs on local communities without any consultation—frequently with unsatisfactory results, since the programs all too often turned out to be unsuitable for the local landscape or culture. Farmers all over the world, for instance, have been advised, lectured, and even paid by outside "experts" to adopt new planting techniques, only to abandon them shortly thereafter in favor of their more appropriate traditional practices.[88]

**More than 60 national constitutions recognize a responsibility to protect the environment.**

When the local people actually get to be involved in the formulation of a project, however, they can mold it to their needs, and it is much more likely to succeed. Community involvement also has the potential to serve as a direct deterrent to the abuse of environmental human rights. It is a fundamental principle of moral philosophy, after all, that bridging the gap between decisions and their consequences increases the likelihood that the decisions will be moral. When the people who will be directly affected by pollution or natural resource extraction are sitting at the same decision-making table as industry representatives and government officials, development is more likely to proceed in an ecologically sensitive manner: developers can no longer ignore the impact of their projects.[89]

While community-based conservation often works best when initiated by the community itself, policymakers—even those working at the broadest international levels—can do a lot to spur such initiatives. And many national governments, along with the major institutions funding development programs, have already made significant investments in a new participatory approach. Both the World Bank and the United States Agency for International Development (USAID), for example, recently released participation action plans, which lay out their intention to involve communities

affected by their development projects in designing, imple-
menting, and evaluating those projects.[90]

Over and over again, participatory programs have
proven to be excellent tools in the promotion of environmentally sound, equitable development. In western Africa,
for instance, a government-sponsored program called Land
Resource Management on the Central Plateau in Burkina
Faso (PATECORE) has dramatically improved the lives of
farmers living in 240 marginal villages—thanks to program
officers who conducted systematic surveys to find out what
sort of agricultural assistance the farmers themselves
desired. PATECORE has succeeded because it made the farmers' participation part of an ongoing process, so that program activities could be continually adapted to varying field
conditions. In some areas, farmers covered the land with
miniature dams and embankments and other small-scale
irrigation devices they designed themselves; elsewhere, they
spread rich manure composts over previously unfertilized
crops. After just a few years, they had transformed 10,000
hectares of previously unproductive drylands, and the average family's food deficit of 645 kilograms per year had
turned into a 150-kilogram surplus.[91]

Of course, community members cannot be full partici-
pants in development schemes unless their internationally
recognized right to information is respected. And they cannot make good decisions about their future unless they have
access to the full body of scientific literature relating to any
environmental threats they might encounter—unless they
know all of their options and the likely consequences of
each one. From a policy standpoint, guaranteeing this particular set of procedural rights will involve both spurring
governments and corporations to make full disclosures of
their activities, and empowering citizens to educate themselves about their local landscape and to conduct their own
environmental audits and investigations.[92]

One promising means of increasing institutional transparency is community right-to-know legislation, pioneered
by the United States in the 1986 Emergency Planning and

Community Right-to-Know Act and several related laws. Under this type of legislation, in the United States and a few other countries, governments must furnish a wide array of environmental data, make proposed environmental laws available for public comment, publish information regarding failure to comply with environmental laws, and provide information detailing environmental enforcement procedures. In Mexico City, for instance, under the provisions of the North American Free Trade Agreement, the Mexican government's National Institute of Ecology each day monitors and reports local air pollution levels.[93]

Getting national governments to pass and comply with such laws, however, especially in countries governed by rights-repressive regimes, will take considerable international pressure both from other countries and from watchdog organizations. And getting corporations to comply with environmental laws and live up to the same standards of transparency applied to governments in right-to-know legislation will be yet another formidable task. Official policies can certainly help make companies accountable for their environmental records, though. The World Bank, for instance, now requires developers to do an environmental impact statement before beginning work on most Bank-funded projects. Even though the standards for the impact statement remain vague, its existence at least provides a first check against environmental damage.[94]

In the United States, the push for more transparency that led the government to embrace communities' right to information also had a significant impact on the corporate world. One of the most important results of the Emergency Planning and Community Right-to-Know Act was the creation of the Toxics Release Inventory (TRI), an annual computerized record of about 300 toxic chemicals released into the environment by more than 24,000 industrial facilities. American manufacturers, in addition, must now file a Materials Safety Data Sheet, disclosing to employees the substances to which they might be exposed and how that exposure could potentially affect their health. Thanks to the TRI,

citizens of Northfield, Minnesota, working closely with ana-
lysts from the Natural Resources Defense Council (NRDC),
discovered in 1987 that a local electronics firm was emitting
large amounts of the suspected carcinogen methylene chlo-
ride. They were thus able to attach hard data to claims that
their health was being compromised. Public pressure forced
the company, Sheldahl, Inc., to agree to sharp emissions
reductions as part of a renegotiated union contract.[95]

Perhaps the best way to make potential polluters
accountable for their actions is to enable the neighboring
community to participate directly in the monitoring and
reporting process. The community of Manchester, Texas,
learned this lesson the hard way in 1992, after an accident
at the local Rhône-Poulenc chemical plant landed 27 people
in the hospital. But the citizens' subsequent legal challenge
to the company's hazardous waste permit could serve as an
extremely important precedent. The legally binding agreement they made with Rhône-Poulenc required the company
to disclose all of its environment-related documents, and,
more importantly, to pay for a comprehensive environmental audit by an independent outside expert—to be accompanied and overseen by representatives of the community, the
plant's work force, and a local environmental organization
called Texans United.[96]

Development programs stressing community efforts to
gather and process environmental information are often
excellent safeguards against abuses of those communities'
rights. Land-use mapping projects run by groups as diverse
as the rubber tappers on the Chico Mendes Extractive
Reserve and the Nunavik Inuit Indians on land they own in
northern Canada have helped prevent illegal incursions by
loggers and hunters and have facilitated the development of
management plans to ensure equitable, sustainable harvests.
In the western United States, the federal government's
Bureau of Indian Affairs has initiated a program to train tribal governments to use computerized Geographic Information Systems (GIS), which could provide reliable data that
would dramatically improve the Indians' ability to defend

themselves in ongoing disputes over land and water rights. And in a small Andean village in southern Colombia, research undertaken by a group of farmers, with the aid of a visiting anthropologist, proved that local water shortages previously believed to have resulted from dry weather were in fact caused by the redirection of streams by large landowners. The farmers used their findings to mobilize their community and mount a successful campaign to get their water back.[97]

Some communities that have used participatory information-gathering strategies to protect themselves against environmental injustices have even initiated training programs for other at-risk communities. Early in 1995, for example, with the support of the International Development Research Center (a Canadian NGO), a few native technicians from the Split Lake Cree community, having already established their own monitoring program to ensure the safety of their drinking water, travelled to Chile and taught bacteriological water-testing skills to two bands of Mapuche Indians. Projects like this one, linking two small communities in two different hemispheres, suggest both the broad scope of environmental problems and the broad applicability of human-rights solutions to those problems.[98]

## Toward Environmental Justice

"The environment is man's first right."

> — Ken Saro-Wiwa, leader of the Movement for the
> Survival of Ogoni People, in a letter which friends
> smuggled out of his Nigerian prison cell and
> which was read by his son in San Francisco at the
> award ceremony for the Goldman Environmental
> Prize in April 1995[99]

In the end, environmental justice is such a powerful concept because it brings everyone to the same level—that of shared dependence on an intact, healthy environment. The potential coalition surrounding environmental justice issues, in other words, is immense: everyone is willing to fight for something like clean water. As people become aware that environmentally destructive practices threaten everyone's health and livelihood—not even the world's elites will be able to insulate themselves from global warming—they often stop taking the environment for granted or thinking of it as a luxury. They come to see it instead as fundamental to their survival—a basic human right.

No activists will ever achieve any kind of justice if citizens cannot participate in key decisions—if the people in power have dictatorial authority to determine what justice means. But if human rights activists and environmentalists choose to collaborate, and focus their efforts on the issues they share in common, and uphold the universal right to a healthy environment through the free exercising of civil and political rights, their power to change the status quo will likely increase dramatically.

The universal human rights framework provides all individuals with a practical means of defending themselves against environmental degradation. Environmentalists are good at coming up with scientifically sound ways of reducing pollution and slowing resource depletion, but they need human rights activists to uphold people's ability to get such reforms implemented.

Both human rights and environmental agreements have been crucial in coordinating global efforts to combat environmental degradation. But the older, better-established human rights covenants are especially well designed to unite vastly different cultures in this common struggle. As then-Secretary-General of the U.N. Javier Pérez de Cuéllar asserted in 1987, international human rights law "has equal relevance and validity for every political or social system and also every cultural tradition. It can be truly said to belong to the peoples of the world." The different countries of the world will probably never agree on a definition of environmental justice. And yet they have already agreed to protect the basic human rights that make achieving environmental justice a very real possibility.[100]

If all the vulnerable members of society—the impoverished, indigenous peoples, ethnic minorities, women, children—had access to environmental information and could exercise their right to free speech, if they had a voice in determining their own future access to resources, then potential polluters and profligate consumers would no longer be able to treat them as expendable and would have to seek alternatives to their polluting activities and their overconsumption.

Environmentalists often talk about prevention, about the importance of reducing pollution at the source and simply avoiding ecological damage rather than having to deal with its consequences. It is easier and more efficient to cope with hazardous waste by producing less of it, for example, than by finding more places to dump it. What environmentalists have learned from human rights activists is that confronting the dumpers with the dumped-on is the best preventive measure of all. Protecting the rights of the most vulnerable members of our society, in other words, is perhaps the best way we have of protecting the right of future generations to inherit a planet that is still worth inhabiting.

# Notes

**1.** Quoted in Susanna Hecht and Alexander Cockburn, *The Fate of the Forest: Developers, Destroyers, and Defenders of the Amazon* (New York: Harper Collins, 1990).

**2.** Marlise Simons, "Brazilian Who Fought to Protect Amazon Is Killed," *New York Times*, December 24, 1988; Andrew Revkin, *The Burning Season: The Murder of Chico Mendes and the Fight for the Amazon Rain Forest* (New York: Plume, 1990); Hecht and Cockburn, op. cit. note 1.

**3.** Revkin, op. cit. note 2; land-related murders from Amnesty International, *Brazil Briefing* (New York: 1988).

**4.** Acre land distribution from Revkin, op. cit. note 2, and from Stephan Schwartzman, "Land Distribution and the Social Costs of Frontier Development in Brazil: Social and Historical Context of Extractive Reserves," in Daniel C. Nepstad and Stephan Schwartzman, eds., *Non-Timber Products from Tropical Forests: Evaluation of a Conservation and Development Strategy—Advances in Economic Botany*, Vol. 9 (New York: The New York Botanical Garden, 1992); similar trends are documented in Hecht and Cockburn, op. cit. note 1, in Marianne Schmink and Charles H. Wood, *Contested Frontiers in Amazonia* (New York: Columbia University Press, 1992), and in Erick G. Highum and Karen Parker, "Development, Rights, and the Rainforests," *Peace Review*, Fall 1994.

**5.** Hecht and Cockburn, op. cit. note 1; Revkin, op. cit. note 2; James K. Boyce, "Inequality as a Cause of Environmental Degradation," *Ecological Economics*, Vol. 11, 1994, pp. 169-178; Barbara Rose Johnston, ed., *Who Pays the Price? The Sociocultural Context of Environmental Crisis* (Washington, D.C.: Island Press, 1994); on the human rights approach, see Michael J. Kane, "Promoting Political Rights to Protect the Environment," *The Yale Journal of International Law*, Winter 1993.

**6.** Bunyan Bryant, ed., *Environmental Justice: Issues, Policies, Solutions* (Washington, D.C.: Island Press, 1995); Richard Hofrichter, ed., *Toxic Struggles: The Theory and Practice of Environmental Justice* (Philadelphia: New Society Publishers, 1993); James K. Boyce, "Equity and the Environment: Social Justice Today as a Prerequisite for Sustainability in the Future," *Alternatives*, Vol. 21, No.1, 1995; Robert D. Bullard, ed., *Unequal Protection: Environmental Justice and Communities of Color* (San Francisco: Sierra Club Books, 1994); attacks against individuals from "Activists at Risk in US and Abroad," *Earth Island Journal*, Summer 1995.

**7.** Road and dam projects from The World Bank, Environment Department, *Resettlement and Development: The Bankwide Review of Projects Involving Involuntary Resettlement, 1986-1993* (Washington, D.C.: 1994); hazardous waste from Jennifer R. Kitt, "Waste Exports to the Developing World: A Global Response," *The Georgetown International Environmental Law*

*Review*, Vol. 7, 1995, pp. 485-514, and from Jennifer Clapp, *Dumping on the Poor: The Toxic Waste Trade with Developing Countries*, Occasional Paper No. 5 (Cambridge, U.K.: University of Cambridge, Global Security Programme, 1994); Narmada from Human Rights Watch/Asia, "Before the Deluge: Human Rights Abuses at India's Narmada Dam," *News from Asia Watch*, June 17, 1992, and from "Sardar Sarovar Project: Review of Resettlement and Rehabilitation in Maharashtra," *Economic and Political Weekly*, August 21, 1993; South Africa from Alan B. Durning, *Apartheid's Environmental Toll*, Worldwatch Paper 95 (Washington, D.C.: Worldwatch Institute, May 1990).

**8.** Hecht and Cockburn, op. cit. note 1; I. Foster Brown et al., "Empowering Local Communities in Land-Use Management: The Chico Mendes Extractive Reserve, Acre, Brazil," *Cultural Survival Quarterly*, Winter, 1995; Stephan Schwartzman, "Extractive Reserves: The Rubber Tappers' Strategy for Sustainable Use of the Amazon Rainforest," in John O. Browder, ed., *Fragile Lands of Latin America: Strategies for Sustainable Development* (Boulder: Westview Press, 1989); Philip M. Fearnside, "Extractive Reserves in Brazilian Amazonia: An Opportunity to Maintain Tropical Rain Forest under Sustainable Use," *BioScience*, June 1989; John O. Browder, "The Limits of Extractivism: Tropical Forest Strategies Beyond Extractive Reserves," *BioScience*, March 1992; on defining environmental justice, see United States Environmental Protection Agency, Office of Environmental Justice, *Environmental Justice Strategy: Executive Order 12898* (Washington, D.C.: 1995).

**9.** Kane, op. cit. note 5; Amartya Sen, "Freedoms and Needs: An Argument for the Primacy of Political Rights," *The New Republic*, January 10 and 17, 1994; Human Rights Watch, *Indivisible Human Rights: The Relationship of Political and Civil Rights to Survival, Subsistence and Poverty* (New York: 1992); on the former Soviet Union, see Barbara Rose Johnston, "The Abuse of Human Environmental Rights: Experience and Response," in Johnston, op. cit. note 5, and Hilary F. French, *Green Revolutions: Environmental Reconstruction in Eastern Europe and the Soviet Union*, Worldwatch Paper 99 (Washington, D.C.: Worldwatch Institute, 1990).

**10.** Audrey R. Chapman, "Earth Rights and Responsibilities: Human Rights and Environmental Protection—Symposium Overview," *The Yale Journal of International Law*, Winter 1993; Kerry Kennedy Cuomo, "Human Rights and the Environment: Common Ground," *The Yale Journal of International Law*, Winter 1993; Margaret Keck and Kathryn Sikkink, "International Issue Networks in the Environment and Human Rights," paper prepared for the XVII International Congress of the Latin American Studies Association, Los Angeles, September 24-27, 1992.

**11.** Paul Leicester Ford, ed., *The Writings of Thomas Jefferson*, Vol. 10 (New York: G.P. Putnam's Sons, 1899).

**12.** Chris Kiefer and Medea Benjamin, "Solidarity with the Third World: Building an International Environmental Justice Movement," in Hofrichter, op. cit. note 6; Chapman, op. cit. note 10.

**13.** Quote from Ashish Kothari, Indian Institute of Public Administration, New Delhi, private communication, July 25, 1995; Chipko movement from Vandana Shiva and J. Bandyopdhyay, "The Evolution, Structure, and Impact of the Chipko Movement," *Mountain Research Development* 6, 1986, pp. 133-42, from Chandi Prasad Bhatt, "Chipko Movement: The Hug That Saves," *The Hindu Survey of the Environment 1991* (Madras: 1991), and from Vikram Akula, "Grassroots Environmental Resistance in India," in Bron Raymond Taylor, ed., *Ecological Resistance Movements: The Global Emergence of Radical and Popular Environmentalism* (Albany: State University of New York Press, 1995).

**14.** United Church of Christ Commission for Racial Justice, *Toxic Wastes and Race in the United States: A National Report on the Racial and Socio-Economic Characteristics of Communities with Hazardous Waste Sites* (New York: 1987); environmental justice studies listed and summarized in Benjamin A. Goldman, *Not Just Prosperity: Achieving Sustainability with Environmental Justice* (Washington, D.C.: National Wildlife Federation, 1993); see also Citizens' Clearinghouse for Hazardous Wastes, *Ten Years of Triumph* (Arlington, Virginia: 1993), and United States Environmental Protection Agency, Office of Policy, Planning, and Evaluation, *Environmental Equity: Reducing Risk for All Communities—Volume 2: Supporting Document* (Washington, D.C.: 1992).

**15.** Yale conference from American Association for the Advancement of Science and Yale Law School, *Earth Rights and Responsibilities: Human Rights and Environmental Protection—Conference Report* (New Haven: Yale Law School, 1992); Human Rights Watch (HRW) and Natural Resources Defense Council (NRDC), *Defending the Earth: Abuses of Human Rights and the Environment* (Washington, D.C.: 1992); Nigeria letter from Stephen Mills, International Program, Sierra Club, Washington, D.C., private communication, October 13, 1995.

**16.** Chapman, op. cit. note 10.

**17.** Michael Posner, "Rally Round Human Rights," *Foreign Policy*, Winter 1994-95; Fali S. Nariman, "The Universality of Human Rights," *International Commission of Jurists—The Review*, No. 50, 1993; Jack Donnelly, "Human Rights in the New World Order," *World Policy Journal*, Spring 1992; Center for the Study of Human Rights, Columbia University, *Twenty-Five Human Rights Documents* (New York: 1994).

**18.** Kane, op. cit. note 5; Chapman, op. cit. note 10; Cuomo, op. cit. note 10; Keck and Sikkink, op. cit. note 10; HRW and NRDC, op. cit. note 15; Sangita Wilk-Sanatani, "Lessons Learned at the World Conference on Human Rights," *Environmental Conservation*, Autumn 1993; Ferdinando Albanese, "Towards a New Human Right?" *Naturopa*, No. 70, 1992; Dinah Shelton, "Human Rights, Environmental Rights, and the Right to

Environment," *Stanford Journal of International Law*, Vol. 28, 1991, pp. 103-138; Adriana Fabra Aguilar and Neil A. F. Popovic, "Lawmaking in the United Nations: The UN Study on Human Rights and the Environment," *Reciel*, Vol. 3, No. 4, 1994.

**19.** Aguilar and Popovic, op. cit. note 18; Paul G. Harris, "Global Equity and Sustainable Development," *Peace Review*, Fall 1994.

**20.** Rodrigues quoted (in translation) in Hecht and Cockburn, op. cit. note 1; on the missing human component in wilderness preservation, see Arturo Gomez-Pompa and Andrea Kaus, "Taming the Wilderness Myth," *BioScience*, April 1992; Margaret E. Keck, "Parks, People and Power: The Shifting Terrain of Environmentalism," *NACLA Report on the Americas*, March/April 1995; "When Conservation is not Enough: Bringing the Community Back into View," *Surviving Together*, Spring 1995; Jules N. Pretty and Michael P. Pimbert, "Beyond Conservation Ideology and the Wilderness Myth," *Natural Resources Forum*, Vol. 19, No. 1, 1995; and Michael Wells and Katrina Brandon with Lee Hannah, *People and Parks: Linking Protected Area Management with Local Communities* (Washington, D.C.: World Bank, 1992).

**21.** Masai from Pretty and Pimbert, op. cit. note 20; India's protected areas from Ashish Kothari, Saloni Suri, and Neena Singh, "Protected Areas in India: A New Beginning," *Economic and Political Weekly*, forthcoming, from Sarbani Sarkar, Neena Singh, Saloni Suri, and Ashish Kothari, *Joint Management of Protected Areas in India: Report of a Workshop* (New Delhi: Indian Institute of Public Administration, 1995), and from Neena Singh and Ashish Kothari, "Balancing Act: The Interim Report on Rajaji National Park," *Frontline*, June 30, 1995; Kutru Tiger and Buffalo Reserve from Pretty and Pimbert, op. cit. note 20.

**22.** Tyua woman from Robert K. Hitchcock, "International Human Rights, the Environment, and Indigenous Peoples," *Colorado Journal of International Environmental Law and Policy*, Winter 1994.

**23.** Revkin, op. cit. note 2; Cuomo, op. cit. note 10; Wilk-Sanatani, op. cit. note 18.

**24.** Holmes Rolston, III, "Rights and Responsibilities on the Home Planet," *The Yale Journal of International Law*, Winter 1993; Galápagos from Bruce Stutz, "The Sea Cucumber War," *Audubon*, May-June 1995, and from Macarena Green, "Crisis in the Galápagos Islands," *Wild Lands Advocate*, April 1995.

**25.** Richard Stone, "Fishermen Threaten Galápagos," *Science*, February 3, 1995; James Brooke, "Ban on Harvesting Sea Cucumber Pits Scientists Against Fishermen," *New York Times*, November 2, 1993; Valle quote from Stutz, op. cit. note 24.

26. Linda Rabben, "Kayapó Choices: Short-term Gain vs. Long-term Damage," *Cultural Survival Quarterly*, Summer 1995; Brian Homewood, "Brazilian Court Bans Indians from 'Mining' Mahogany," *New Scientist*, July 22, 1995; Matt Moffett, "Kayapó Indians Lose Their 'Green' Image," *Wall Street Journal*, December 29, 1994.

27. Hitchcock, op. cit. note 22; Alan Thein Durning, *Guardians of the Land: Indigenous Peoples and the Health of the Earth*, Worldwatch Paper 112 (Washington, D.C.: Worldwatch Institute, December 1992).

28. Revkin, op. cit. note 2; Keck and Sikkink, op. cit. note 10.

29. Revkin, op. cit. note 2; Schwartzman, op. cit. note 8; Fearnside, op. cit. note 8; Browder, op. cit. note 8; Stephan Schwartzman and Mary Helena Allegretti, "Extractive Production in the Amazon and the Rubber Tappers' Movement," paper published by Environmental Defense Fund, Washington, D.C., May 28, 1987.

30. Quoted in David Helvarg, *The War Against the Greens: The "Wise Use" Movement, the New Right, and Anti-Environmental Violence* (San Francisco: Sierra Club Books, 1994).

31. HRW and NRDC, op. cit. note 15.

32. Tarahumara, Fernandez, and Dara from *Earth Island Journal*, op. cit. note 6; additional information on Dara from Amnesty International, "Kingdom of Cambodia: Human Rights and the New Government," March 14, 1995; Russia from Joshua Handler, Greenpeace, Washington, D.C., letter to U.S. Vice-President Albert Gore, October 11, 1995. Table 1 is drawn from the following: Kozhevnikov from HRW and NRDC, op. cit. note 15; D'Achille from Kane, op. cit. note 5; Domoldol from HRW and NRDC, op. cit. note 15, and from Rainforest Action Network, "Philippine Rainforest Leader Murdered," Action Alert #64, September 1991; Mehta from "Harnessing the Law to Clean up India," *Multinational Monitor*, July/August 1995, and from "Delhi's Green Warrior," *Asiaweek*, August 25, 1995; Pence from Jim Robbins, "Target Green: Federal Land Managers under Attack," *Audubon*, July-August 1995, and from "Forest Ranger Becomes Target of 2 Bombings," *New York Times*, August 6, 1995.

33. Maathai from Cuomo, op. cit. note 10, and from Mary Ann French, "The Woman and Mother Earth," *Washington Post*, June 2, 1992; Mojica from HRW and NRDC, op. cit. note 15; Greece from Vassilios Katsoupas, World Wide Fund for Nature, WWF Greece, private communication, November 8, 1995.

34. David Helvarg, "Property Rights and Militias: The Anti-Enviro Connection," *The Nation*, May 22, 1995; Helvarg, op. cit. note 30.

35. Helvarg, op. cit. note 30.

**36.** Timothy Lynch, *Polluting Our Principles: Environmental Prosecutions and the Bill of Rights*, Policy Analysis Paper No. 223 (Washington, D.C.: Cato Institute, 1995).

**37.** "The Goldman Environmental Prize Winners for 1995," *Earth Island Journal*, Summer 1995; Raymond Bonner, "Trying to Document Rights Abuses," *New York Times*, July 26, 1995.

**38.** "1994 Right Livelihood Awards Stress Importance of Children, Spiritual Values, and Indigenous Cultures," press release by Michelle Syverson and Associates, Manzanita, Oregon, December 1994; Charles McCoy, "Goldman Environmental Prizes Likely to Go to California Woman, Nigerian," *Wall Street Journal*, April 17, 1995.

**39.** Cited in Robert D. Bullard, ed., *Confronting Environmental Racism: Voices from the Grassroots* (Boston: South End Press, 1993).

**40.** Johnston, op. cit. note 5.

**41.** Ibid.

**42.** Ken Saro-Wiwa, "Stand by Me and the Ogoni People," *Earth Island Journal*, Summer 1995; Human Rights Watch/Africa, "Nigeria: The Dawn of a New Dark Age," New York, October 1994; "Government in Nigeria Accused of Repression," *Financial Times*, November 11, 1994; "Nigerian Oil Activist on Trial," *The Ecologist*, January/February 1995; "Persecution of Ken Saro-Wiwa," *New African*, May 1995; Environmental Defense Fund, "Environment, Human Rights Groups Demand Niger Delta Cleanup," Washington, D.C., May 26, 1995; "Nigeria: Saro-Wiwa Sentenced to Death; Enviros Outraged," *Greenwire—The Environmental News Daily*, November 1, 1995; Stephen Buckley, "Nigeria Hangs Playwright, Eight Activists— International Pleas for Mercy Ignored," *Washington Post*, November 11, 1995.

**43.** Steve Kretzmann, "Nigeria's 'Drilling Fields'," *Multinational Monitor*, January/February 1995; Geraldine Brooks, "Slick Alliance: Shell's Nigerian Fields Produce Few Benefits for Region's Villagers," *Wall Street Journal*, May 6, 1994.

**44.** Kretzmann, op. cit. note 43; Brooks, op. cit. note 43.

**45.** Kretzmann, op. cit. note 43; Brooks, op. cit. note 43.

**46.** Afton from Robert D. Bullard, *Dumping in Dixie: Race, Class, and Environmental Quality* (Boulder: Westview Press, 1990), from Robert M. Frye, "Environmental Injustice: The Failure of American Civil Rights and Environmental Law to Provide Equal Protection from Pollution," *Dickinson Journal of Environmental Law and Policy*, Fall 1993, and from Barbara Rose Johnston, "The Abuse of Human Environmental Rights: Experience and

Response," in Johnston, op. cit. note 5. Table 2 is drawn from the following: Udege from Anjali Acharya, "The Fate of the Boreal Forests," *World Watch*, May/June 1995, and from Kevin Schafer and Martha Hill, "The Logger and the Tiger," *Wildlife Conservation*, May/June 1993; Wales from "Opencast Miners Plunder Wales," *The Ecologist*, January/February 1995; Yami from Global Response, "GRAction #6/95, Nuclear Waste Dumping—Environmental Racism/Taiwan," Boulder, September 8, 1995, and from "The Stink on Orchid Island," *The Economist*, August 26, 1995; Ecuador from Thomas S. O'Connor, "'We Are Part of Nature': Indigenous Peoples' Rights as a Basis for Environmental Protection in the Amazon Basin," *Colorado Journal of International Environmental Law and Policy*, Winter 1994, from David Holmstrom, "Texaco Has Left Ecuador, But Its Impact Remains," *Christian Science Monitor*, March 25, 1994, and from Enrique Yeves, "Mud, Stench, and Rotor-Whop," *Ceres*, March-April 1994; Malawi from Bill Derman and Anne Ferguson, "Human Rights, Environ-ment, and Development: Dispossession of Fishing Communities on Lake Malawi," in Johnston, op. cit. note 5.

**47.** Barbara Rose Johnston and Susan Dawson, "Resource Use and Abuse on Native American Land: Uranium Mining in the American Southwest," in Johnston, op. cit. note 5.

**48.** Johnston and Dawson, op. cit. note 47; Joseph G. Jorgenson, "The Political Economy of the Native American Energy Business," in Jorgenson, ed., *Native Americans and Energy Development II* (Boston: Anthropology Research Center, 1984).

**49.** Johnston and Dawson, op. cit. note 47; Catherine Caulfield, *Multiple Exposures: Chronicles of the Radiation Age* (Toronto: Stoddart, 1989); M. J. Samet et al., "Uranium Mining and Lung Cancer among Navajo Men," *New England Journal of Medicine*, Vol. 310, 1984, pp. 1481-1484.

**50.** Audrey R. Topping, "Ecological Roulette: Damming the Yangtze," *Foreign Affairs*, September/October 1995; Lena H. Sun, "Dam Could Alter Face of China," *Washington Post*, December 31, 1991; Fred Pearce, "The Biggest Dam in the World," *New Scientist*, January 25, 1995.

**51.** Sandra Burton, "Taming the River Wild," *Time*, December 19, 1994; Kuwait's population from Population Reference Bureau (PRB), *1995 World Population Data Sheet* (Washington, D.C.: 1995); study by Chinese Academy of Sciences from Pearce, op. cit. note 50.

**52.** Human Rights Watch/Asia, "The Three Gorges Dam in China: Forced Resettlement, Suppression of Dissent, and Labor Rights Concerns," New York, February 1995; Dai Qing, *Yangtze! Yangtze!* (London: Earthscan, 1994).

**53.** The World Bank, op. cit. note 7.

**54.** David Western and R. Michael Wright, eds., *Natural Connections:*

*Perspectives in Community-based Conservation* (Washington, D.C.: Island Press, 1994); John Friedmann and Haripriya Rangan, eds., *In Defense of Livelihood: Comparative Studies on Environmental Action* (West Hartford, Conn.: Kumarian Press, 1993); Charlie Pye-Smith and Grazia Borrini Feyerabend with Richard Sandbrook, *The Wealth of Communities: Stories of Success in Local Environmental Management* (West Hartford, Conn.: Kumarian Press, 1994); Christine Meyer and Faith Moosang, eds., *Living with the Land: Communities Restoring the Earth* (Philadelphia: New Society Publishers, 1992). Table 3 is drawn from the following: India from Vithal Rajan, "Power of the Poor," *Resurgence*, September/October 1994; Yanesha from Manuel Lázaro, Mario Pariona, and Robert Simeone, "A Natural Harvest," *Cultural Survival Quarterly*, Spring 1993; Egypt from Laila Kamel, "Learning from the Poor," *Earth Island Journal*, Summer 1994; California from Michael Corbett, "California Tribe Wins Control of Native Lands and Plans Nature Park," *Christian Science Monitor*, April 5, 1995; Nepal from Vijayalakshmi Balakrishnan, "Trekking to Balanced Development," *Down to Earth*, August 15, 1992, and from Michael P. Wells, "A Profile and Interim Assessment of the Annapurna Conservation Area Project, Nepal," in Western and Wright, op. cit. this note; Kakadu from M.A. Hill and A.J. Press, "Kakadu National Park: An Australian Experience in Comanagement," in Western and Wright, op. cit. this note.

55. Pye-Smith and Feyerabend with Sandbrook, op. cit. note 54.

56. Ibid.

57. Muhammad Yunus, "New Development Options Towards the 21st Century," Grameen Bank, Dhaka, Bangladesh, undated; Manfred A. Max-Neef, *Human Scale Development: Conception, Application, and Further Reflections* (New York: The Apex Press, 1991); Bruce Rich, *Mortgaging the Earth: The World Bank, Environmental Impoverishment, and the Crisis of Development* (Boston: Beacon Press, 1994); Mahbub ul Haq, *Reflections on Human Development* (New York: Oxford University Press, 1995).

58. Harald Hohmann, ed., *Basic Documents of International Environmental Law*, Vol. 1 (London: Graham and Trotman, 1992).

59. The Ecologist, *Whose Common Future: Reclaiming the Commons* (Philadelphia: New Society Publishers, 1993); Wolfgang Sachs, *Global Ecology: A New Arena of Political Conflict* (London: Zed Books, 1993).

60. Hilary F. French, *Partnership for the Planet: An Environmental Agenda for the United Nations*, Worldwatch Paper 126 (Washington, D.C.: Worldwatch Institute, July 1995).

61. World Resources Institute, *World Resources 1994-95* (New York: Oxford University Press, 1994); Jyoti Parikh et al., "Consumption Patterns: The Driving Force of Environmental Stress," Indira Gandhi Institute of Development Research Discussion Paper No. 59, Bombay, 1991.

**62.** PRB, op. cit. note 51; Alan Durning, *How Much Is Enough? The Consumer Society and the Future of the Earth* (New York: W.W. Norton & Company, 1992).

**63.** WRI, op. cit. note 61; John E. Young, *Mining the Earth*, Worldwatch Paper 109 (Washington, D.C.: Worldwatch Institute, July 1992).

**64.** Kitt, op. cit. note 7; Clapp, op. cit. note 7; Greenpeace, "Database of Known Hazardous Waste Exports from OECD to non-OECD Countries, 1989-March 1994," Washington, D.C., March 1994, paper prepared for the Second Conference of Parties to the Basel Convention, Geneva, March 21-25, 1994; United Nations Environment Programme, "Generation of Hazardous Wastes and Other Wastes, 1993 Statistics," paper prepared for the Third Meeting of the Conference of the Parties to the Basel Convention, Geneva, September 18-22, 1995.

**65.** Clapp, op. cit. note 7; Third World Network, *Toxic Terror: Dumping of Hazardous Wastes in the Third World* (Penang, Malaysia: 1989).

**66.** Examples drawn from Clapp, op. cit. note 7.

**67.** Kitt, op. cit. note 7; "Hazardous Waste: Countries Developing List of Materials That Would Fall under Proposed Trade Ban," *International Environment Reporter*, July 26, 1995; U.S. figure from Clapp, op. cit. note 7.

**68.** Barbara Rose Johnston and Gregory Button, "Human Environmental Rights Issues and the Multinational Corporation: Industrial Development in the Free Trade Zone," in Johnston, op. cit. note 5; Philip F. Coppinger, "Mexico's *Maquiladoras*: Economic Boon and Social Crisis," *New Solutions*, Spring 1993; Louis Head and Michael Guerrero, "Fighting Environmental Racism," *New Solutions*, Spring 1991; Jeannie Ralston, "Among the Ruins of Matamoros," *Audubon*, November-December 1993; Lynda Yanz, "Women's *Maquila* Network: Mexico to Central America," *Correspondencia*, May 1994; Tod Robberson, "Mexicans Say Cleanup of Border Imperiled," *Washington Post*, May 16, 1995; GAO study from Nancy Dunne, "Negligent Neighbors," *Financial Times*, May 12, 1993; compliance with 1983 agreement from June Juffer, "Dump at the Border: U.S. Firms Make a Mexican Wasteland," *The Progressive*, October 1988, and from Bill Moyers, *Global Dumping Ground: The International Traffic in Hazardous Waste* (Washington, D.C.: Seven Locks Press, 1990).

**69.** Johnston and Button, op. cit. note 68; Hilary F. French, *Costly Tradeoffs: Reconciling Trade and the Environment*, Worldwatch Paper 113 (Washington, D.C.: Worldwatch Institute, March 1993); Esther Schrader, "A Giant Spraying Sound: Since NAFTA, Mexican Growers Are Spraying More Toxic Pesticides on Fruit, Vegetables, and Workers," *Mother Jones*, January/February 1995; Tim Lang and Colin Hines, "GATT: A Disaster for the Environment, Rural Economies, Food Quality, and Food Security," *Ceres*, January-February 1995; Barbara Dinham, ed., *The Pesticide Hazard: A*

*Global Health and Environmental Audit* (London: Zed Books, 1993).

**70.** Consumption figure from Barbara Dinham, ed., *The Pesticide Trail: The Impact of Trade Controls on Reducing Pesticide Hazards in Developing Countries* (London: The Pesticides Trust, January 1995); poisonings and deaths from Jumanah Farah, *Pesticide Policies in Developing Countries: Do They Encourage Excessive Use?* World Bank Discussion Paper 238 (Washington, D.C.: The World Bank, 1994).

**71.** Free-trade law from Barbara Dinham, "The Potential of Prior Informed Consent," *Global Pesticide Campaigner*, August 1993 (Washington, D.C.: Pesticide Action Network); GAO study from U.S. General Accounting Office, "Export of Unregistered Pesticides Is Not Adequately Monitored by EPA," Washington, D.C., April 1989; poisonings estimate from J. Jeyaratnam, "Acute Pesticide Poisoning: A Major Problem," *World Health Statistics Quarterly*, Vol. 43, 1990, pp. 139-144; Peru's population from PRB, op. cit. note 51; FAO study from Food and Agriculture Organization, *Analysis of Government Responses to the First Questionnaire on the International Code of Conduct on the Distribution and Use of Pesticides* (Rome: 1993).

**72.** Dinham, *The Pesticide Hazard*, op. cit. note 69; David Pearce et al., "Debt and the Environment," *Scientific American*, June 1995; Will Nixon, "Relief Disaster," *In These Times*, August 22, 1994; Gianni Vaggi, ed., *From the Debt Crisis to Sustainable Development: Changing Perspectives on North-South Relations* (New York: St. Martin's Press, 1993); Jessica Vivian, *Social Safety Nets and Adjustment in Developing Countries*, UNRISD Occasional Paper Series, No. 1 (Geneva: United Nations Research Instititue for Sustainable Development, July 1994); Derrick K. Gondwe, *Political Economy, Ideology, and the Impact of Economics on the Third World* (New York: Praeger Publishers, 1992).

**73.** Gary Lee, "Proposal to Log Suriname's Rain Forest Splits the Needy Nation," *Washington Post*, May 13, 1995; Anthony DePalma, "In Suriname's Rain Forests, A Fight Over Trees vs. Jobs," *New York Times*, September 4, 1995.

**74.** Lee, op. cit. note 73; Russell A. Mittermeier, "Economic Crisis in Suriname Threatens Ecological Eden," *Christian Science Monitor*, April 19, 1995.

**75.** The Human Rights Council of Australia, Inc., *The Rights Way to Development: A Human Rights Approach to Development Assistance* (Sydney: 1995); Iglesias's letter from Lee, op. cit. note 73, and from Nigel Sizer, "Suriname's Fire Sale," *New York Times*, May 14, 1995.

**76.** Russell A. Mittermeier, "What Costa Rica Can Teach Suriname," *Wall Street Journal*, September 1, 1995; Mittermeier, op. cit. note 74.

**77.** Industrial emissions from Atiq Rahman, Nick Robins, and Annie

Roncerel, eds., *Exploding the Population Myth: Consumption Versus Population—Which Is the Climate Bomb?* (Brussels: Climate Network Europe, 1993); U.S.-India comparison from Christopher Flavin, "Facing up to the Risks of Climate Change," in Lester R. Brown, et al., *State of the World 1996* (New York: W. W. Norton, forthcoming, 1996).

**78.** Flavin, op. cit. note 77.

**79.** Hilary F. French, *After the Earth Summit: The Future of Environmental Governance*, Worldwatch Paper 107 (Washington, D.C.: Worldwatch Institute, March 1992); Richard Elliot Benedick, *Ozone Diplomacy* (Cambridge, Mass.: Harvard University Press, 1991).

**80.** Howard B. Furer, ed., *Lyndon B. Johnson, 1908-: Chronology, Documents, Bibliographical Aids* (Dobbs Ferry, N.Y.: Oceana Publications, Inc., 1971).

**81.** Aguilar and Popovic, op. cit. note 18.

**82.** Human Rights Council of Australia, op. cit. note 75.

**83.** Aguilar and Popovic, op. cit. note 18; "The 1994 Draft Declaration of Principles on Human Rights and the Environment," Geneva, 1994; Commission on Human Rights, Sub-Commission on Prevention of Discrimination and Protection of Minorities, *Human Rights and the Environment: Final Report*, prepared by Ms. Fatma Zohra Ksentini, Special Rapporteur, Forty-sixth session, Item 4 of the provisional agenda, July 6, 1994; "Resolution on Human Rights and the Environment," *Environmental Law Network International Newsletter*, February 1995; Allan McChesney, "Linking Human Rights, Environment, and Sustainability," *ECODECISION*, Winter 1995; Günter Hoog and Angela Steinmetz, eds., *International Conventions on Protection of Humanity and Environment* (New York: Walter de Gruyter Publishers, 1993).

**84.** Center for the Study of Human Rights, op. cit. note 17; Aguilar and Popovic, op. cit. note 18; Albanese, op. cit. note 18; French, op. cit. note 79; Commission on Human Rights, op. cit. note 83; Hoog and Steinmetz, op. cit. note 83; Kristi N. Rea, "Linking Human Rights and Environmental Quality," in Lawrence E. Susskind, William R. Moomaw, and Adil Najam, eds., *Papers on International Environmental Negotiation*, Vol. 4 (Cambridge, Mass.: The Program on Negotiation at Harvard Law School, 1994).

**85.** Aguilar and Popovic, op. cit. note 18; Rea, op. cit. note 84; Amnesty International, *Summary of Selected International Procedures and Bodies Dealing with Human Rights Matters* (New York: August 1989); Hurst Hannum, ed., *Guide to International Human Rights Practice* (Philadelphia: University of Pennsylvania Press, 1984); Susan E. Brice, "Convention on the Rights of the Child: Using a Human Rights Instrument to Protect Against Environmental Threats," *The Georgetown International Environmental Law Review*, Vol. 7, 1995, pp. 587-611.

**86.** Aguilar and Popovic, op. cit. note 18; Commission on Human Rights, Sub-Commission on Prevention of Discrimination and Protection of Minorities, Forty-fourth session, July 2, 1992, Item 4 of the provisional agenda, Human Rights and the Environment, Progress Report prepared by Mrs. Fatma Zohra Ksentini; Neil Popovic, International Program, Sierra Club Legal Defense Fund, San Francisco, Calif., private communication, October 12, 1995.

**87.** National and regional mechanisms from Commission on Human Rights, op. cit. note 83, and from Commission on Human Rights, op. cit. note 86; Ecuador from World Bank, *Ecuador Judicial Sector Assessment*, Report No. 12777-EC (Washington, D.C.: August 1994), and from Victoria C. Arthaud, "Environmental Destruction in the Amazon: Can U.S. Courts Provide a Forum for the Claims of Indigenous People?" *The Georgetown International Environmental Law Review*, Vol. 7, 1995, pp. 195-233.

**88.** On the International Covenant on Civil and Political Rights, see Center for the Study of Human Rights, op. cit. note 17; on Agenda 21 and the Vienna Declaration, see Commission on Human Rights, op. cit. note 83; on participation in general, see Nici Nelson and Susan Wright, *Power and Participatory Development: Theory and Practice* (London: Intermediate Technology Publications, 1995).

**89.** Judith Plant and Christopher Plant, *Putting Power in its Place: Create Community Control!* (Philadelphia: New Society Publishers, 1992); Camilla Toulmin, "Empowering the People," *Our Planet*, Vol. 6, No. 5, 1994; Anisur Rahman, *People's Self-Development: Perspectives on Participatory Action Research—A Journey Through Experience* (London: Zed Books, 1994).

**90.** The World Bank, Operations Policy Department, *The World Bank and Participation* (Washington, D.C.: 1994); Nancy C. Alexander, Bread for the World Institute, Testimony on the World Bank, Poverty, and Popular Participation, to the Banking Subcommittee on Domestic and International Monetary Affairs, U.S. House of Representatives, Washington, D.C., March 27, 1995; The Honorable J. Brian Atwood, U.S. Agency for International Development, "Statement of Principles on Participatory Development," Washington, D.C., November 16, 1993.

**91.** Burkina Faso from Fiona Hinchcliffe, Irene Guijt, Jules N. Pretty, and Parmesh Shah, *New Horizons: The Economic, Social, and Environmental Impacts of Participatory Watershed Development*, Gatekeeper Series No. 50 (London: International Institute for Environment and Development, 1995).

**92.** The right to information is recognized in the International Covenant on Civil and Political Rights, Article 19; see Center for the Study of Human Rights, op. cit. note 17, and Commission on Human Rights, op. cit. note 83.

**93.** The Environmental Law Reporter, *Community Right-to-Know Deskbook* (Washington, D.C.: Environmental Law Institute, 1988); Mexico from Mark

J. Spalding, "Resolving International Environmental Disputes: Public Participation and the Right-to-Know," *Journal of Environment and Development*, Winter 1995.

**94.** David Sarokin, "A Proposal to Create a Corporate Social Environmental Impact Statement," *New Solutions*, Spring 1995; World Bank from Nancy C. Alexander, op. cit. note 90.

**95.** Environmental Law Reporter, op. cit. note 93; U.S. Environmental Protection Agency, Office of Pollution Prevention and Toxics, *1993 Toxics Release Inventory: Public Data Release* (Washington, D.C.: 1995); Sheldahl from Randolph B. Smith, "Right to Know: A U.S. Report Spurs Community Action by Revealing Polluters," *Wall Street Journal*, January 2, 1991, and from "Union, Citizens Push for Reductions," *Working Notes on Community Right-to-Know*, Working Group on Community Right to Know, Washington, D.C.; July 1990.

**96.** Sanford Lewis, "Moving Forward Toward Environmental Excellence: Corporate Environmental Audits, Disclosure, and Stakeholder Empowerment," *New Solutions*, Spring 1995.

**97.** Chico Mendes Extractive Reserve from Brown et al., op. cit. note 8; Nunavik Inuit Indians from William B. Kemp and Lorraine F. Brooke, "Towards Information Self-Sufficiency: The Nunavik Inuit Gather Information on Ecology and Land Use," *Cultural Survival Quarterly*, Winter 1995; GIS from Michael E. Marchand and Richard Winchell, "Tribal Implementation of GIS: A Case Study of Planning Applications with the Colville Confederated Tribes," *Cultural Survival Quarterly*, Winter 1994, and from Theodore S. Glickman, "Measuring Environmental Equity with Geographical Information Systems," *Renewable Resources Journal*, Autumn 1994; Colombia from International Development Research Centre, "Colombian Farmers Conduct Own Research," *Leads*, April 1995.

**98.** International Development Research Centre, "Northern Manitoba Band Teaches Water-Testing Skills to Chileans," *Leads*, April 1995.

**99.** Saro-Wiwa, op. cit. note 42.

**100.** Pérez de Cuéllar quote from Amnesty International, op. cit. note 85.

# PUBLICATION ORDER FORM

No. of
Copies

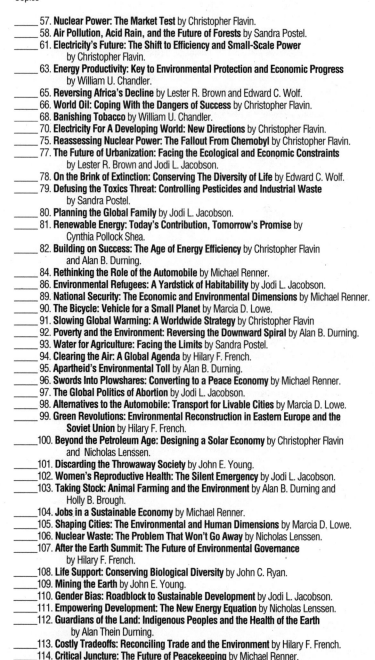

_____ 57. **Nuclear Power: The Market Test** by Christopher Flavin.
_____ 58. **Air Pollution, Acid Rain, and the Future of Forests** by Sandra Postel.
_____ 61. **Electricity's Future: The Shift to Efficiency and Small-Scale Power**
         by Christopher Flavin.
_____ 63. **Energy Productivity: Key to Environmental Protection and Economic Progress**
         by William U. Chandler.
_____ 65. **Reversing Africa's Decline** by Lester R. Brown and Edward C. Wolf.
_____ 66. **World Oil: Coping With the Dangers of Success** by Christopher Flavin.
_____ 68. **Banishing Tobacco** by William U. Chandler.
_____ 70. **Electricity For A Developing World: New Directions** by Christopher Flavin.
_____ 75. **Reassessing Nuclear Power: The Fallout From Chernobyl** by Christopher Flavin.
_____ 77. **The Future of Urbanization: Facing the Ecological and Economic Constraints**
         by Lester R. Brown and Jodi L. Jacobson.
_____ 78. **On the Brink of Extinction: Conserving The Diversity of Life** by Edward C. Wolf.
_____ 79. **Defusing the Toxics Threat: Controlling Pesticides and Industrial Waste**
         by Sandra Postel.
_____ 80. **Planning the Global Family** by Jodi L. Jacobson.
_____ 81. **Renewable Energy: Today's Contribution, Tomorrow's Promise** by
         Cynthia Pollock Shea.
_____ 82. **Building on Success: The Age of Energy Efficiency** by Christopher Flavin
         and Alan B. Durning.
_____ 84. **Rethinking the Role of the Automobile** by Michael Renner.
_____ 86. **Environmental Refugees: A Yardstick of Habitability** by Jodi L. Jacobson.
_____ 89. **National Security: The Economic and Environmental Dimensions** by Michael Renner.
_____ 90. **The Bicycle: Vehicle for a Small Planet** by Marcia D. Lowe.
_____ 91. **Slowing Global Warming: A Worldwide Strategy** by Christopher Flavin
_____ 92. **Poverty and the Environment: Reversing the Downward Spiral** by Alan B. Durning.
_____ 93. **Water for Agriculture: Facing the Limits** by Sandra Postel.
_____ 94. **Clearing the Air: A Global Agenda** by Hilary F. French.
_____ 95. **Apartheid's Environmental Toll** by Alan B. Durning.
_____ 96. **Swords Into Plowshares: Converting to a Peace Economy** by Michael Renner.
_____ 97. **The Global Politics of Abortion** by Jodi L. Jacobson.
_____ 98. **Alternatives to the Automobile: Transport for Livable Cities** by Marcia D. Lowe.
_____ 99. **Green Revolutions: Environmental Reconstruction in Eastern Europe and the
         Soviet Union** by Hilary F. French.
_____100. **Beyond the Petroleum Age: Designing a Solar Economy** by Christopher Flavin
         and Nicholas Lenssen.
_____101. **Discarding the Throwaway Society** by John E. Young.
_____102. **Women's Reproductive Health: The Silent Emergency** by Jodi L. Jacobson.
_____103. **Taking Stock: Animal Farming and the Environment** by Alan B. Durning and
         Holly B. Brough.
_____104. **Jobs in a Sustainable Economy** by Michael Renner.
_____105. **Shaping Cities: The Environmental and Human Dimensions** by Marcia D. Lowe.
_____106. **Nuclear Waste: The Problem That Won't Go Away** by Nicholas Lenssen.
_____107. **After the Earth Summit: The Future of Environmental Governance**
         by Hilary F. French.
_____108. **Life Support: Conserving Biological Diversity** by John C. Ryan.
_____109. **Mining the Earth** by John E. Young.
_____110. **Gender Bias: Roadblock to Sustainable Development** by Jodi L. Jacobson.
_____111. **Empowering Development: The New Energy Equation** by Nicholas Lenssen.
_____112. **Guardians of the Land: Indigenous Peoples and the Health of the Earth**
         by Alan Thein Durning.
_____113. **Costly Tradeoffs: Reconciling Trade and the Environment** by Hilary F. French.
_____114. **Critical Juncture: The Future of Peacekeeping** by Michael Renner.

\_\_\_\_\_115. **Global Network: Computers in a Sustainable Society** by John E. Young.

\_\_\_\_\_116. **Abandoned Seas: Reversing the Decline of the Oceans** by Peter Weber.

\_\_\_\_\_117. **Saving the Forests: What Will It Take?** by Alan Thein Durning.

\_\_\_\_\_118. **Back on Track: The Global Rail Revival** by Marcia D. Lowe.

\_\_\_\_\_119. **Powering the Future: Blueprint for a Sustainable Electricity Industry**
by Christopher Flavin and Nicholas Lenssen.

\_\_\_\_\_120. **Net Loss: Fish, Jobs, and the Marine Environment** by Peter Weber.

\_\_\_\_\_121. **The Next Efficiency Revolution: Creating a Sustainable Materials Economy**
by John E. Young and Aaron Sachs.

\_\_\_\_\_122. **Budgeting for Disarmament: The Costs of War and Peace** by Michael Renner.

\_\_\_\_\_123. **High Priorities: Conserving Mountain Ecosystems and Cultures**
by Derek Denniston.

\_\_\_\_\_124. **A Building Revolution: How Ecology and Health Concerns Are Transforming
Construction** by David Malin Roodman and Nicholas Lenssen.

\_\_\_\_\_125. **The Hour of Departure: Forces That Create Refugees and Migrants** by Hal Kane.

\_\_\_\_\_126. **Partnership for the Planet: An Environmental Agenda for the United Nations**
by Hilary F. French.

——127. **Eco-Justice: Linking Human Rights and the Environment** by Aaron Sachs.

\_\_\_\_\_ **Total Copies**

**Single Copy: $5.00** • 2–5: $4.00 ea. • 6–20: $3.00 ea. • 21 or more: $2.00 ea.
Call Director of Communication at (202) 452-1999 to inquire about discounts on larger orders.

☐ **Membership in the Worldwatch Library: $30.00 (international airmail $45.00)**
The paperback edition of our 250-page "annual physical of the planet,"
*State of the World,* plus all Worldwatch Papers released during the calendar year.

☐ **Subscription to *World Watch* magazine: $20.00 (international airmail $35.00)**
Stay abreast of global environmental trends and issues with our award-winning, eminently readable bimonthly magazine.

---

☐ **Worldwatch Database Disk Subscription: One year for $89**
Includes current global agricultural, energy, economic, environmental, social, and military indicators from all current Worldwatch publications. Includes a mid-year update, and *Vital Signs* and *State of the World* as they are published. Can be used with Lotus 1-2-3, Quattro Pro, Excel, SuperCalc and many other spreadsheets.
Check one: \_\_\_\_\_high-density IBM-compatible or \_\_\_\_\_Macintosh

---

**Make check payable to Worldwatch Institute**
1776 Massachusetts Avenue, N.W., Washington, D.C. 20036-1904 USA

*Please include $3 postage and handling for non-subscription orders.*

Enclosed is my check for U.S. $_____
AMEX ☐  VISA ☐  Mastercard ☐ _____

|  |  |
|---|---|
| Card Number | Expiration Date |

---

**name**                                            **daytime phone #**

---

**address**

---

**city**                                       **state**         **zip/country**

**Phone: (202) 452-1999**     **Fax: (202) 296-7365**     **E-Mail: wwpub@igc.apc.org**     WW

# PUBLICATION ORDER FORM

No. of
Copies

_____ 57. **Nuclear Power: The Market Test** by Christopher Flavin.

_____ 58. **Air Pollution, Acid Rain, and the Future of Forests** by Sandra Postel.

_____ 61. **Electricity's Future: The Shift to Efficiency and Small-Scale Power**
by Christopher Flavin.

_____ 63. **Energy Productivity: Key to Environmental Protection and Economic Progress**
by William U. Chandler.

_____ 65. **Reversing Africa's Decline** by Lester R. Brown and Edward C. Wolf.

_____ 66. **World Oil: Coping With the Dangers of Success** by Christopher Flavin.

_____ 68. **Banishing Tobacco** by William U. Chandler.

_____ 70. **Electricity For A Developing World: New Directions** by Christopher Flavin.

_____ 75. **Reassessing Nuclear Power: The Fallout From Chernobyl** by Christopher Flavin.

_____ 77. **The Future of Urbanization: Facing the Ecological and Economic Constraints**
by Lester R. Brown and Jodi L. Jacobson.

_____ 78. **On the Brink of Extinction: Conserving The Diversity of Life** by Edward C. Wolf.

_____ 79. **Defusing the Toxics Threat: Controlling Pesticides and Industrial Waste**
by Sandra Postel.

_____ 80. **Planning the Global Family** by Jodi L. Jacobson.

_____ 81. **Renewable Energy: Today's Contribution, Tomorrow's Promise** by
Cynthia Pollock Shea.

_____ 82. **Building on Success: The Age of Energy Efficiency** by Christopher Flavin
and Alan B. Durning.

_____ 84. **Rethinking the Role of the Automobile** by Michael Renner.

_____ 86. **Environmental Refugees: A Yardstick of Habitability** by Jodi L. Jacobson.

_____ 89. **National Security: The Economic and Environmental Dimensions** by Michael Renner.

_____ 90. **The Bicycle: Vehicle for a Small Planet** by Marcia D. Lowe.

_____ 91. **Slowing Global Warming: A Worldwide Strategy** by Christopher Flavin

_____ 92. **Poverty and the Environment: Reversing the Downward Spiral** by Alan B. Durning.

_____ 93. **Water for Agriculture: Facing the Limits** by Sandra Postel.

_____ 94. **Clearing the Air: A Global Agenda** by Hilary F. French.

_____ 95. **Apartheid's Environmental Toll** by Alan B. Durning.

_____ 96. **Swords Into Plowshares: Converting to a Peace Economy** by Michael Renner.

_____ 97. **The Global Politics of Abortion** by Jodi L. Jacobson.

_____ 98. **Alternatives to the Automobile: Transport for Livable Cities** by Marcia D. Lowe.

_____ 99. **Green Revolutions: Environmental Reconstruction in Eastern Europe and the
Soviet Union** by Hilary F. French.

_____100. **Beyond the Petroleum Age: Designing a Solar Economy** by Christopher Flavin
and Nicholas Lenssen.

_____101. **Discarding the Throwaway Society** by John E. Young.

_____102. **Women's Reproductive Health: The Silent Emergency** by Jodi L. Jacobson.

_____103. **Taking Stock: Animal Farming and the Environment** by Alan B. Durning and
Holly B. Brough.

_____104. **Jobs in a Sustainable Economy** by Michael Renner.

_____105. **Shaping Cities: The Environmental and Human Dimensions** by Marcia D. Lowe.

_____106. **Nuclear Waste: The Problem That Won't Go Away** by Nicholas Lenssen.

_____107. **After the Earth Summit: The Future of Environmental Governance**
by Hilary F. French.

_____108. **Life Support: Conserving Biological Diversity** by John C. Ryan.

_____109. **Mining the Earth** by John E. Young.

_____110. **Gender Bias: Roadblock to Sustainable Development** by Jodi L. Jacobson.

_____111. **Empowering Development: The New Energy Equation** by Nicholas Lenssen.

_____112. **Guardians of the Land: Indigenous Peoples and the Health of the Earth**
by Alan Thein Durning.

_____113. **Costly Tradeoffs: Reconciling Trade and the Environment** by Hilary F. French.

_____114. **Critical Juncture: The Future of Peacekeeping** by Michael Renner.

\_\_\_\_\_ **Total Copies**

**Single Copy: $5.00** • 2–5: $4.00 ea. • 6–20: $3.00 ea. • 21 or more: $2.00 ea.
Call Director of Communication at (202) 452-1999 to inquire about discounts on larger orders.

☐ **Membership in the Worldwatch Library: $30.00 (international airmail $45.00)**
The paperback edition of our 250-page "annual physical of the planet,"
*State of the World,* plus all Worldwatch Papers released during the calendar year.

☐ **Subscription to *World Watch* magazine: $20.00 (international airmail $35.00)**
Stay abreast of global environmental trends and issues with our award-winning,
eminently readable bimonthly magazine.

☐ **Worldwatch Database Disk Subscription: One year for $89**
Includes current global agricultural, energy, economic, environmental, social, and
military indicators from all current Worldwatch publications. Includes a mid-year
update, and *Vital Signs* and *State of the World* as they are published. Can be used
with Lotus 1-2-3, Quattro Pro, Excel, SuperCalc and many other spreadsheets.
Check one: \_\_\_\_\_high-density IBM-compatible or \_\_\_\_\_Macintosh

**Make check payable to Worldwatch Institute**
1776 Massachusetts Avenue, N.W., Washington, D.C. 20036-1904 USA

*Please include $3 postage and handling for non-subscription orders.*

Enclosed is my check for U.S. $_____

AMEX ☐  VISA ☐  Mastercard ☐  _____
                                    Card Number                              Expiration Date

**name**                                                          **daytime phone #**

**address**

**city**                                              **state**        **zip/country**

**Phone: (202) 452-1999   Fax: (202) 296-7365      E-Mail: wwpub@igc.apc.org**